# The Currency of Peace

Paul Frank

ARMIDEP

Copyright © 2024 by Paul Frank

All rights reserved.

No portion of this book may be reproduced in any form without written permission from the publisher or author, except as permitted by U.S. copyright law.

# Contents

| | |
|---|---|
| Dedication | V |
| Preface | VI |
| Introduction | VII |
| 1. The Illusion of External Peace | 1 |
| 2. The Body's Wisdom | 20 |
| 3. The Impact of Relationships on Inner Peace | 39 |
| 4. Finding Your True Calling | 63 |
| 5. The Nature of Attachment | 86 |
| 6. The Spirit Within | 103 |
| 7. The Interconnectedness of Peace | 118 |
| 8. Meditation and Mindfulness | 135 |
| 9. The Inevitability of Challenges | 156 |
| 10. The Currency of Peace: A legacy of Tranqulity | 170 |
| Acknowledgments | 182 |
| Appendix | 184 |
| Glossary | 188 |

Author Biography 190

## Dedication

This book is dedicated to all those seeking a deeper sense of peace, both within themselves and in the world around them. May these words serve as a guiding light on your journey to inner harmony and lasting fulfillment.

# **PREFACE**

In a world clamoring for attention, consumed by external pursuits, and often burdened by inner turmoil, we forget the true treasure that lies within us: peace. This is not the fleeting peace of a moment's respite but the profound, enduring tranquility that resides deep within our hearts, waiting to be discovered and cultivated.

"The Currency of Peace" is a testament to the power of inner peace. It is a self-help guide and a journey of exploration, discovery, and transformation. Through its pages, we will delve into the depths of our being, uncovering the internal conflicts that hinder our peace, and learn practical tools and wisdom to achieve true harmony.

This book is for you, the seeker, the yearning heart, the individual who recognizes that true peace is the foundation of a meaningful and joyful life. It is a compass to guide you through the storms of life, offering a sense of calm, clarity, and purpose.

Let us embark on this transformative journey together, unlocking the boundless potential for peace within us all.

# INTRODUCTION

Imagine a world free from inner turmoil, where anxiety is a distant memory, and contentment flows effortlessly. This is the realm of inner peace, a state of being that transcends the limitations of material possessions, external validation, and even the absence of conflict.

Inner peace is not a destination but a journey. It is a continual practice of self-awareness, mindful living, and a deep connection to our inner source. It is about embracing our emotions, nurturing our bodies, and aligning our actions with our values and purpose.

In our pursuit of happiness, we often seek it in the external world – in relationships, achievements, and material wealth. However, true happiness springs from within, cultivated through inner peace. It is a state of being that radiates outward, influencing our relationships, work, and impact on the world.

This book is your invitation to embark on this journey of inner exploration. It is a roadmap, a collection of wisdom, and practical tools to guide you towards a life of lasting peace and fulfillment.

Within these pages, you will discover the power of:

1. **Calming the mind:** Techniques for quieting negative thoughts and anxieties

2. **Nurturing the body:** Practices for promoting physical well-being

3. **Building peaceful relationships:** Skills for cultivating empathy, communication, and forgiveness

4. **Discovering purpose:** Tools for finding your true calling and aligning your actions with your values

5. **Letting goes of attachments and fears:** Strategies for releasing anxieties and embracing acceptance

6. **Connecting to your spiritual source:** Practices for deepening your connection to a higher power

Through engaging narratives, practical insights, and real-world examples, this book invites you to explore the profound impact of inner peace on all aspects of your life.

Are you ready to embrace the journey to peace? Let's begin.

# 1

## THE ILLUSION OF EXTERNAL PEACE

The world often whispers a seductive lie: that peace is found outside us, in the embrace of material possessions, the warmth of fulfilling relationships, or the validation of social status. We chase these elusive treasures, convinced that acquiring them will usher in a state of serenity. But what we find is a bittersweet paradox.

Imagine a young man driven by the desire for wealth. He works tirelessly, sacrificing sleep and leisure, believing that the accumulation of riches will bring him peace. Yet, as his bank account swells, he finds himself consumed by anxiety. He worries about losing what he's earned, fearing that his fortune might vanish like a wisp of smoke. The relentless pursuit of more only intensifies his internal turmoil.

Similarly, a woman may yearn for a profound love that will erase all her anxieties. She dives headfirst into relationships, hoping to find solace in another's embrace. Initially, passion and connection bring a sense of fulfillment. However, as time unfolds, the weight of expectations, the inevitable conflicts, and the fear of losing the connection can leave her feeling more isolated and insecure than before.

We seek peace in the external, believing that the right job, the perfect home, or the ideal partner will be the key to unlocking a life of tranquility. Yet, the truth lies in a more profound and elusive place: within us.

The illusion of external peace is a deceptive mirage, a shimmering oasis in the desert of our desires. It offers fleeting moments of contentment, leaving us yearning for more. Like a hungry traveler lured by a mirage, we chase these fleeting promises, only to discover that true peace lies not in acquiring external things but in cultivating our inner landscape.

The quest for external peace is often fueled by a deep-seated fear of uncertainty, fear of lack, fear of loss. We clutch onto material possessions, relationships, and social status, believing that these external anchors will provide us with a sense of security. However, the truth is that these external dependencies can become shackles, binding us to a state of constant anxiety and dissatisfaction.

Consider the individual who spends countless hours at the gym, obsessed with achieving the perfect physique. They believe that a sculpted body will bring them acceptance, admiration, and peace. However, pursuing the ideal often becomes a relentless cycle of self-criticism and dissatisfaction. The constant comparison to others and the pressure to conform to societal standards can lead to feelings of inadequacy and a lack of true self-acceptance.

Or imagine a couple who meticulously curate their social media presence, showcasing their seemingly perfect lives to the world. They strive to project an image of happiness and success, hoping that external validation will bring them inner peace. However, this facade of perfection often masks deeper insecurities and anxieties. The constant need to compare themselves to others and seek approval can lead to feelings of isolation, envy, and a disconnection from their true selves.

This pursuit of external peace is often rooted in a fundamental misunderstanding of what peace truly is. We associate peace with the absence of conflict, the cessation of suffering, or achieving a particular outcome. Yet, peace is not simply the absence of something; it is the presence of something far more profound: a state of deep, enduring tranquility that transcends the ups and downs of life.

True peace is not a destination to be reached but a state of being to be cultivated. It is not a fleeting emotion, but a fundamental aspect of our nature, waiting to be discovered and nurtured. A wellspring of tranquility resides within us, waiting to be tapped into.

It is like the quiet hum of a gentle breeze, a sense of calm that pervades our being, a gentle whisper that speaks of our inherent connection to something larger than ourselves. It is the stillness that remains when the storm has passed, the quiet confidence that arises from knowing that the ebb and flow of external circumstances does not define us.

The quest for peace is a journey inward, a profound exploration of our inner landscape. It is a journey of self-discovery, a process of unraveling the intricate web of our thoughts, emotions, and beliefs that shape our experience of the world.

As we embark on this inner odyssey, we will discover that the external world merely reflects our internal state. The peace we seek lies not in the acquisition of things but in the transformation of our minds, our hearts, and our spirits.

It is a journey that demands courage, patience, and a willingness to let go of our attachments to the illusion of external peace. It is a journey that invites us to embrace the present moment, cultivate mindfulness, and connect with the source of peace that resides within each of us.

The path to inner peace is not a straight line but a winding road filled with twists and turns, moments of joy and despair, and the constant opportunity for growth. It is a journey that unfolds in the quiet moments of introspection, during life's challenges, and in the depths of our own hearts.

We often seek peace outside ourselves—in material possessions, relationships, social status, or even in the absence of conflict. We chase after fleeting moments of calm, hoping to achieve a sense of tranquility that never truly sticks. But what if the key to lasting peace lies not in external circumstances but within our own hearts and minds?

Imagine a still pond reflecting the beauty of the world around it. The surface appears peaceful, but beneath the tranquil surface lies a constant current of activity. This is how we often experience life, seeking peace in the stillness of the moment while our internal world is filled with restless thoughts and emotions. We chase external peace, hoping to find calm amidst the chaos, but true peace resides within, untouched by the storms of the outer world.

Inner peace is not a fleeting feeling or a temporary state of mind but a profound and enduring tranquility that emanates from within. It's not the absence of conflict or stress but the ability to remain centered and serene amidst life's inevitable challenges. The quiet strength allows us to weather any storm, a wellspring of resilience that empowers us to face adversity with grace and composure.

Think of a lighthouse standing strong against the crashing waves, its steady beam guiding ships through the darkness. This is the essence of inner peace—an unwavering presence that shines through the storms of life. The calm within the chaos, the unwavering beacon, guides us through difficult times.

Pursuing inner peace is not about escaping life's challenges; it's about finding a deeper sense of stability and clarity within us, allowing us to navigate life's complexities with greater ease and grace. It's about cultivating an inner sanctuary, a place of refuge where we can find solace and renewal, even when the world around us feels turbulent.

Imagine a serene garden, a haven of tranquility amidst the hustle and bustle of everyday life. The fragrant flowers bloom in vibrant colors, attracting butterflies and hummingbirds, while the gentle breeze rustles the leaves. This is a metaphor for inner peace—a place of beauty, harmony, and tranquility that resides within us, waiting to be cultivated.

Think of it this way: our minds are like a garden. Just as a gardener cultivates the soil, removes weeds, and nurtures the plants, so too must we tend to the garden of our minds. We must cultivate positive thoughts, nourish our emotions, and eliminate negative patterns of thinking that can hinder our peace. By tending to the garden within, we create a haven of inner peace, a sanctuary from the storms of the outer world.

The journey to inner peace begins with a deep understanding of the nature of peace itself. It's not about achieving a state of complete stillness or eliminating all emotions. It's about developing a balanced and resilient mind that can navigate the ups and downs of life with grace and composure. It's about finding a sense of harmony between our thoughts, emotions, and actions, allowing us to live in alignment with our true selves.

Think of a grand orchestra, each instrument playing its own melody, yet all blending together in perfect harmony. This is the essence of inner peace—a symphony of thoughts, emotions, and actions that create a beautiful and harmonious whole. It's the ability to navigate life's complexities with grace and composure, finding balance and serenity amidst the chaos.

In the coming chapters, we will explore the various aspects of cultivating inner peace—from the power of the mind and the importance of physical well-being to the role of relationships and the transformative nature of living a life of purpose. Together, we will embark on a journey of self-discovery, uncovering the hidden wellspring of peace that lies within each of us.

But for now, remember this: the quest for peace is not about escaping life's challenges but finding a deeper sense of stability and clarity within us, allowing us to navigate life's complexities with greater ease and grace. It's about cultivating an inner sanctuary, a place of refuge where we can find solace and renewal, even when the world around us feels turbulent.

The journey to inner peace is within your reach. Take the first step today. The mind, a powerful engine of our being, plays a crucial role in shaping our experience of peace. It's a complex landscape of thoughts, beliefs, and emotions, constantly churning, shaping, and influencing our inner state. Just as a skilled gardener cultivates a flourishing garden, we must learn to cultivate a peaceful mind.

Imagine your mind as a vast garden, with vibrant flowers representing positive thoughts, nourishing the soul with joy and serenity. But weeds, those intrusive negative thoughts, can quickly overgrow, casting shadows on our inner peace. Nurtured by fear, worry, anger, and self-doubt, these weeds can choke out the beauty and serenity within.

Like the soil in our mental garden, our beliefs provide the foundation for our thoughts and emotions. If our beliefs are rooted in negativity, self-criticism, and lack, the soil becomes infertile, making it difficult for positive thoughts to flourish. But if our beliefs are nourished with self-acceptance, compassion, and gratitude, the soil becomes fertile, allowing seeds of peace to take root and blossom.

Emotions, like the weather patterns in our mental garden, can bring both sunshine and storms. Positive emotions like love, joy, and contentment create a warm and nurturing climate, promoting growth and peace. Conversely, negative emotions like anger, fear, and sadness act as harsh storms, disrupting our inner harmony and hindering our ability to experience peace.

Negative thoughts, often fueled by our beliefs, can cloud our minds and hinder our ability to experience peace. They can be intrusive, relentless, and seemingly impossible to stop. We may find ourselves trapped in a cycle of self-criticism, worry, or fear, creating a state of constant inner turmoil.

Consider the example of a person struggling with anxiety. They may constantly replay negative thoughts about the future, fearing the unknown and dwelling on potential threats. These thoughts can spiral out of control, leading to physical symptoms like a racing heart, shallow breathing, and muscle tension. This constant mental chatter creates an internal storm that prevents them from finding peace and tranquility.

Another example is someone battling self-doubt. They may constantly compare themselves to others, questioning their abilities and worthiness. These thoughts can create feelings of inadequacy and insecurity, hindering them from pursuing their passions and achieving their full potential.

Just as farmers must diligently weed their fields, we must actively tend to our mental garden, nurturing positive thoughts and beliefs while uprooting negative ones. This involves becoming aware of our thoughts, challenging negative thought patterns, and replacing them with more positive and constructive ones.

The journey of cultivating a peaceful mind is a lifelong endeavor, requiring patience, perseverance, and consistent effort. But the rewards are immeasurable, leading to a sense of inner harmony, emotional well-being, and a deep-seated peace that transcends external circumstances.

Here are some techniques to help us cultivate a peaceful mind:

**Mindfulness:** Practice mindfulness through meditation, yoga, or simply taking moments throughout the day to focus on your breath and the present moment. This helps us become aware of our thoughts and emotions without judgment, allowing us to observe and let go of negative patterns.

**Positive Self-Talk:** Replace negative self-talk with positive affirmations and encouraging self-messages. Challenge those critical voices in your head and replace them with words of kindness, acceptance, and encouragement.

**Gratitude Practice:** Cultivate a habit of gratitude by reflecting on the blessings in your life, both big and small. This helps shift your focus from what you lack to what you have, fostering contentment and appreciation.

**Cognitive Reframing:** When negative thoughts arise, challenge their validity. Ask yourself: "Is this thought truly true? Is there another way to look at this situation?" By reframing negative thoughts, you can find more balanced and constructive perspectives.

**Acceptance and Non-Judgment:** Embrace the concept of acceptance, recognizing that you cannot control every situation or outcome. Learn to let go of resistance and embrace the present moment as it is, without judgment.

**Emotional Regulation:** Learn to identify and manage your emotions in healthy ways. This might involve practicing deep breathing exercises, engaging in physical activity, or seeking support from a therapist or counselor.

**Setting Boundaries:** Protect your mental and emotional well-being by setting clear boundaries with others. Learn to say "no" to commitments that drain your energy or contribute to your stress.

**Seeking Support:** Don't be afraid to reach out for help when you need it. Talk to trusted friends, family members, or professionals who can offer support and guidance.

Cultivating a peaceful mind is not about achieving perfection but about embarking on a journey of self-discovery, growth, and transformation. It's a continuous process of awareness, self-compassion, and commitment to nurturing our inner landscape. By tending to our thoughts, beliefs, and emotions, we create a sanctuary of peace within ourselves, allowing us to experience life with greater serenity, joy, and fulfillment.

Imagine a world where your mind's relentless chatter quiets down, replaced by a stillness so profound that it feels like you've stepped into a sanctuary. In this sanctuary, anxieties melt away, worries dissolve, and you experience a peace that transcends the storms of daily life. This is the realm of the present moment, a place where time stands still, and the beauty of existence unfolds in its purest form.

Embracing the present moment is not just about being "in the now" but about cultivating a deep awareness of the richness and wonder surrounding us. It's about noticing the soft caress of the breeze on your skin, the intricate dance of sunlight on leaves, or the quiet hum of a bird's song. It's about savoring the simple joys of life, from the aroma of freshly brewed coffee to the warmth of a loved one's embrace.

But cultivating this mindful presence can feel like an impossible task in a world that's constantly bombarding us with distractions – notifications, emails, deadlines, and endless demands. Our minds are wired to flit from thought to thought, dwelling on the past or worrying about the future, leaving us feeling overwhelmed and disconnected from the present.

However, the good news is that the ability to be present is not something we are born with or without; it's a skill that can be cultivated through conscious practice. Just like a muscle that needs regular exercise, our minds require training to develop the ability to stay anchored in the present.

Here's the beauty of it, the present moment is the only place where true peace resides. It's the ground on which all other forms of peace are built – peace with ourselves, others, and the world around us.

### *The Power of Mindfulness*

Mindfulness is the key to unlocking the treasures of the present moment. It's about paying attention to the here and now without judgment or analysis. It's about observing our thoughts, feelings, and sensations without getting caught up.

When we practice mindfulness, we become more aware of the constant stream of thoughts that flows through our minds, many of which are unnecessary and even harmful. We notice the judgments we make, the worries we cling to, and the negative self-talk that we often engage in.

Mindfulness, however, isn't about suppressing thoughts or trying to force ourselves to be happy all the time. It's about recognizing our thoughts and feelings as fleeting visitors to our minds without giving them the power to control us. It's about creating space between ourselves and our thoughts so that we can choose how to respond to them rather than reacting automatically.

Think of it like a calm observer watching a river flow by. The observer doesn't try to stop the flow of the river; they simply observe its movement, its ripples, its currents, and its occasional eddies. In the same way, we can learn to observe our thoughts and feelings without becoming entangled in them.

### *The Benefits of Presence*

The benefits of living in the present moment are profound and far-reaching. When we learn to stay anchored in the now, we unlock a wealth of inner peace and well-being. Here are a few key benefits:

**Reduced stress and anxiety:** By focusing on the present, we step out of the constant loop of worrying about the past or fretting about the future. This allows us to find a sense of calm and ease, reducing stress and anxiety levels.

**Enhanced emotional regulation:** When we are fully present, we become more aware of our emotions as they arise. We can observe them without getting swept away by them, giving us the space to choose how we want to respond. This allows us to regulate our emotions more effectively and avoid reacting impulsively.

**Increased focus and clarity:** When our minds are not preoccupied with past regrets or future anxieties, we can access a deeper level of focus and clarity. This allows us to be more productive, creative, and present in our interactions with others.

**Greater appreciation for life:** Living in the present allows us to truly appreciate the beauty and wonder surrounding us. We become more aware of the simple joys of life – the smell of fresh-cut grass, the warmth of the sun on our skin, the sound of laughter – and we experience a deeper sense of contentment.

**Strengthened relationships:** When we are present with our loved ones, we can connect with them on a deeper level. We listen more intently, offer genuine empathy, and communicate more clearly. This fosters stronger, more meaningful relationships.

### *The Path to Presence: Practical Tips*

The journey to living in the present moment is a gradual process. It requires patience, compassion, and a willingness to cultivate mindfulness daily. Here are some practical tips to help you get started:

**Start small:** You don't need to attempt to be fully present all the time, especially at the beginning. Start by choosing one activity – eating a meal, taking a walk, having a conversation – and focus on fully engaging in it. Notice the sensations, sights, and sounds, and allow yourself to be fully present in that moment.

**Practice mindful breathing:** Taking a few minutes daily to focus on your breath is a simple yet powerful way to cultivate mindfulness. Sit comfortably, close your eyes, and bring your attention to the rise and fall of your breath. Notice the sensation of the air entering and leaving your nostrils. When your mind wanders, gently guide it back to your breath.

**Engage in mindful activities:** Incorporate mindfulness into your daily routine by practicing mindful walking, eating, or washing dishes. Pay attention to the details of the activity, using your senses to engage fully in the present moment.

**Use meditation:** Meditation is a powerful tool for cultivating mindfulness and accessing a deeper state of presence. There are many different styles of meditation, so find one that resonates with you and start with a few minutes each day. As you become more comfortable, gradually increase the duration of your practice.

**Be patient and compassionate:** The journey to mindfulness is not linear. There will be days when you find it easier to stay present and days when your mind is racing. Be patient with yourself and practice self-compassion. Remember that even a few moments of mindful presence can make a difference.

### *Beyond the Individual: Creating a Collective Presence*

While the pursuit of inner peace is a personal journey, it profoundly impacts the world around us. Cultivating presence within ourselves creates a ripple effect that extends outward, fostering greater harmony and understanding in our relationships and communities.

Imagine a world where people are more mindful of their words and actions, listening with empathy and responding with compassion. Imagine a world where conflict is resolved through open dialogue and understanding, forgiveness replaces resentment, and love becomes the guiding force.

This is the power of collective presence. By embracing the present moment, we transform ourselves and contribute to a more peaceful and harmonious world. It's a journey that starts within each of us and can lead to a brighter and more peaceful future for all.

The quest for peace often leads us to seek it from external sources. We chase material possessions, strive for perfect relationships, and chase societal validation, believing that these things will bring us a sense of contentment and harmony. Yet, these external sources, though enticing, are ultimately fleeting. They offer temporary comfort but cannot deliver the enduring peace we crave. True peace, the kind that transcends external circumstances, resides not in the world outside but within ourselves.

The foundation of this inner peace is a peaceful mind. A mind that is free from constant chatter, rumination, and negative thoughts. A mind that is calm, focused, and present. To cultivate this peaceful mindset, we must first become aware of the thoughts that cloud our peace. We must learn to observe our thoughts without judgment, recognizing them as mere passing clouds in the vast sky of our consciousness. This practice of mindful observation is the first step towards gaining control over our mental state.

Once we become aware of our thoughts, we can begin to challenge the negative ones. Many of our worries are based on assumptions and fears that lack a solid foundation in reality. When we find ourselves caught in a spiral of negativity, we can question the validity of our thoughts. Are they based on facts or imagined scenarios? Do they serve us or hold us back? By questioning our thoughts and reframing them in a more positive light, we can shift our mental landscape from worry and fear to peace and hope.

Beyond observing and challenging negative thoughts, we must also cultivate positive ones. Imagine your mind as a garden. Just as you wouldn't let weeds take over your garden, you wouldn't let negative thoughts overrun your mind. Instead, plant seeds of peace, love, and kindness. These seeds, nurtured through positive affirmations, gratitude practices, and acts of compassion, will blossom into a vibrant garden of inner peace.

One of the most powerful techniques for calming the mind is meditation. Meditation is not about emptying your mind but about training your attention. It is about learning to observe your thoughts without getting carried away by them. Meditation can be practiced in many ways. You can simply sit quietly, focusing on your breath, or you can use guided meditations that lead you through visualizations or affirmations. The key is to find a practice that resonates with you and to be consistent in your practice.

In addition to meditation, there are many other techniques for calming the mind and cultivating a peaceful outlook.

These include:

**Deep breathing exercises:** When we are stressed or anxious, our breathing becomes shallow and rapid. Deep breathing exercises, such as diaphragmatic breathing or box breathing, can help slow our heart rate, lower our blood pressure, and relax our nervous system.

**Mindfulness practices:** Mindfulness involves paying attention to the present moment without judgment. It is about noticing the sensations of your body, the sounds around you, and the thoughts that arise without getting caught up in them. Mindfulness practices can be incorporated into everyday activities, such as eating, walking, or showering, bringing a sense of presence and peace to these simple acts.

**Yoga and movement:** Yoga is a powerful practice that combines physical postures, breathing exercises, and meditation. It helps improve flexibility, strength, and balance while calming the mind and reducing stress. Other forms of movement, such as walking, swimming, or dancing, can promote peace and well-being.

**Spending time in nature:** Nature has a calming effect on the mind and body. Spending time outdoors, whether taking a walk in the park, sitting by a lake, or simply looking at a flower, can help reduce stress and promote a sense of peace.

**Engaging in creative pursuits:** Creative activities, such as painting, drawing, writing, or playing music, can be a powerful way to express ourselves and connect with our inner peace.

The journey to cultivating a peaceful mindset is not a linear path. There will be moments of calm and clarity, and there will be moments of struggle and turmoil. The key is to remember that peace is not a destination but a state of being. It is a continuous process of becoming more aware, compassionate, and aligned with our true selves. By practicing the abovementioned techniques and embracing the journey with patience and kindness, we can gradually cultivate a peaceful mindset that empowers us to navigate life's challenges with grace, resilience, and a deep sense of inner peace.

# 2

## THE BODY'S WISDOM

Our bodies are not merely vessels for our minds and spirits; they are intricately connected to both, forming a delicate and powerful symphony of well-being. To truly understand and experience peace, we must acknowledge and nurture this mind-body connection. It's like a three-legged stool, where each leg represents a different aspect of our being, and all three must be strong and balanced for the stool to stand firm.

If one leg is weak or unstable, the entire stool will wobble.

The mind-body connection is a fundamental principle in many spiritual traditions, recognizing that our thoughts, feelings, and physical states are interconnected. When our bodies are in a state of stress, our minds often follow suit. We might experience racing thoughts, anxiety, and difficulty concentrating. Conversely, when our bodies are relaxed and nourished, our minds tend to be calmer, more focused, and more receptive to peace.

Imagine a beautiful garden where the mind is the gardener, the body is the soil, and the spirit is the flower. The gardener cultivates the soil, ensuring it's rich and fertile with nutrients, allowing the flower to thrive and bloom in its full glory. The flower, in turn, reflects the health of the soil and the gardener's care. Similarly, prioritizing our physical health creates a fertile ground for our minds and spirits to blossom.

Our bodies are constantly sending us signals, communicating their needs and desires. We can gain invaluable insights into our overall well-being if we pay attention to these signals. For instance, when we feel fatigued, it clearly indicates that our bodies need rest and rejuvenation. When we experience digestive issues, it might indicate that our diet needs adjustments.

By paying attention to our physical needs, we can learn to listen to the wisdom of our bodies, understand their language, and respond appropriately. When we cultivate physical well-being, we lay the foundation for a more peaceful and harmonious life.

Here are some key aspects of physical well-being that play a vital role in our journey to inner peace:

**The Power of Movement and Exercise:**

Physical activity is a powerful antidote to stress and anxiety. When we move our bodies, we release endorphins, natural mood boosters that create feelings of happiness and well-being. Exercise also helps to reduce tension, improve sleep quality, and enhance cognitive function. Think of your body like a car. If you park it for too long, it will eventually become rusty and break down. Regular exercise is like taking your car for a spin, keeping it running smoothly and efficiently.

**Nourishing Your Body with Food:**

Our food plays a significant role in our physical and mental health. A balanced diet rich in fruits, vegetables, whole grains, and lean proteins provides the essential nutrients our bodies need to function optimally. Nourishing our bodies with healthy foods promotes energy levels, stabilizes moods, and enhances our cognitive abilities. In contrast, a diet filled with processed foods, refined sugars, and unhealthy fats can lead to fatigue, irritability, and inflammation, creating a fertile ground for mental and emotional distress.

Imagine your body as a temple. What would you offer to a sacred space? Would you bring in junk food and unhealthy treats? Or would you offer it the finest and most nourishing ingredients, honoring its sanctity?

**The Importance of Sleep and Rest:**

Adequate sleep is essential for physical and mental restoration. During sleep, our bodies repair and rebuild tissues, regulate hormones, and consolidate memories. Sleep deprivation can lead to fatigue, irritability, poor concentration, and even an increased risk of chronic diseases. Just like a flower needs sunlight and rain to bloom, our bodies need proper sleep to recharge and flourish.

**Holistic Practices for Physical and Mental Peace:**

Practices like yoga, meditation, and breathwork offer a holistic approach to well-being, integrating physical and mental health for a more balanced and peaceful state. Yoga involves postures and breathing exercises that promote flexibility, strength, and relaxation. Meditation cultivates mindfulness and reduces stress, while deep breathing techniques help to calm the nervous system and reduce anxiety.

These practices can be considered a bridge between our physical and mental realms, creating a harmonious flow of energy and well-being.

Think of your body as a beautiful instrument. If you neglect it, it will become out of tune. By practicing yoga, meditation, and deep breathing, you are learning to play this instrument with grace and skill, creating a symphony of peace within.

Remember, the mind-body connection is a two-way street.

When we cultivate physical well-being, we create a positive feedback loop that supports our mental and emotional health. Conversely, when we focus on our mental and emotional well-being, we can influence our physical health for the better.

By paying attention to the signals our bodies send us, nourishing our bodies with healthy food and exercise, and incorporating practices that promote physical and mental harmony, we create the foundation for a life filled with peace, joy, and fulfillment.

Imagine a world where every step you take is a step towards peace, where your body becomes a vessel for tranquility, and your mind finds clarity and ease in every movement. This is the transformative power of physical activity, a powerful tool for unlocking the body's wisdom and cultivating inner peace.

Our bodies are not merely physical structures; they are interconnected with our minds and spirits, constantly communicating and influencing each other. When we engage in physical activity, we are not only strengthening our muscles and improving our cardiovascular health but also sending signals to our brains that promote a sense of calm and well-being.

One of the most profound benefits of exercise is its ability to reduce stress. When we exercise, our bodies release endorphins, natural mood-boosting chemicals that act as painkillers and create a sense of euphoria. These endorphins help counteract the effects of stress hormones like cortisol, calming our nervous systems and promoting relaxation.

Think of it like this: when you feel overwhelmed, your body is in a state of "fight or flight." Your muscles tense up, your heart beats faster, and your breathing becomes shallow. Exercise helps to break this cycle by redirecting your body's energy and attention. It allows you to release pent-up tension, focus on the present moment, and experience a sense of release and renewal.

Beyond stress reduction, exercise also promotes mental clarity and focus. When you move your body, you also stimulate your brain, increasing blood flow to the prefrontal cortex, the area responsible for executive functions like planning, decision-making, and problem-solving. This increased blood flow and brain activity can lead to enhanced cognitive function, improved memory, and a sharper mind.

Many people find that exercise helps them to think more clearly, solve problems more effectively, and make better decisions. The physical act of movement can also help to clear the mind of racing thoughts and worries, creating space for calmness and creativity to emerge.

The benefits of physical activity extend beyond stress reduction and mental clarity. Exercise can also improve sleep quality, boost your immune system, and increase your overall sense of well-being.

When we engage in regular physical activity, we invest not only in our physical health but also in our emotional, mental, and spiritual well-being. We are acknowledging the interconnectedness of our mind, body, and spirit, tapping into our bodies' inherent wisdom to cultivate a deeper sense of peace and fulfillment.

Think of movement as a form of meditation to connect with your body and your inner self. When you move, whether it be through a brisk walk, a yoga session, or a vigorous workout, you are entering a state of presence and awareness. You are tuning into the rhythm of your breath, the flow of your energy, and the sensations in your body. This mindful movement can help to quiet the mind, release tension, and cultivate a sense of serenity.

You don't need to be a marathon runner or a gym enthusiast to reap the benefits of movement. Even small amounts of physical activity can significantly affect your well-being. Start with a short walk, a few yoga poses, or some simple stretches. Listen to your body, find what feels good, and gradually increase the intensity and duration of your workouts.

As you engage in physical activity, pay attention to the sensations in your body. Notice how your breath deepens, how your muscles relax, and how your mind begins to quiet. This awareness is key to unlocking the body's wisdom and harnessing its transformative power.

The body is a powerful tool for cultivating inner peace, and movement is the key. As you move, you are strengthening your physical form and cultivating a sense of harmony and well-being that extends far beyond your physical body. You are unlocking the wisdom of your body, connecting with your spirit, and embarking on a journey of peace from within.

The link between what we eat and how we feel is profound. Our bodies are intricate machines, and the fuel we provide them directly impacts their performance, including our mental and emotional well-being. Think of it as a delicate dance between the physical and the mental – nourish the body well, and the mind will follow suit, often experiencing a state of greater peace and tranquility. Conversely, neglecting our dietary needs can lead to imbalances that manifest as anxiety, irritability, and even depression.

Imagine a car running on low-grade fuel. It sputters, it lacks power, and it breaks down more frequently. Our bodies operate in a similar manner. If we consistently feed ourselves with processed foods, sugary drinks, and refined carbohydrates, we give our bodies low-grade fuel. Our brains, which require a constant supply of nutrients to function optimally, become sluggish, foggy, and prone to mood swings.

But the good news is that just as high-octane fuel boosts a car, a diet rich in whole, unprocessed foods can dramatically improve our mental state. Imagine a car running on premium fuel, gliding smoothly, with ample power and energy. Our bodies can experience this same transformation when fueled by nutrient-dense foods.

Let's dive into the specific ways our diet can contribute to inner peace:

**The Power of Whole Foods:**

Whole foods are the foundation of a peaceful mind and body.

Think fruits, vegetables, whole grains, lean proteins, and healthy fats. These foods provide our bodies with the essential vitamins, minerals, and antioxidants they need to thrive. They're packed with natural energy, promoting feelings of vitality, focus, and clarity.

**The Role of Blood Sugar Balance:**

When we consume refined carbohydrates and sugary foods, our blood sugar levels spike rapidly, followed by a crash that can trigger feelings of fatigue, irritability, and anxiety. This roller coaster of blood sugar fluctuations can significantly disrupt our inner peace.

However, opting for whole foods like complex carbohydrates found in whole grains, legumes, and fruits, results in a more gradual and sustainable release of energy, keeping our blood sugar levels stable and contributing to a calm, balanced mind.

**The Importance of Gut Health:**

The gut, often called our second brain, is pivotal in our mental and emotional well-being. Recent research has revealed a strong connection between gut and mental health.

A healthy gut microbiome, teeming with beneficial bacteria, promotes a strong immune system, reduces inflammation, and regulates mood. Conversely, an imbalanced gut microbiome, often due to a diet high in processed foods, sugar, and unhealthy fats, can contribute to digestive problems, inflammation, and even mental health issues like anxiety and depression.

**The Power of Hydration:** Water is essential for every bodily function, including our mental clarity and emotional stability. Dehydration can lead to fatigue, headaches, and even feelings of irritability and anxiety.

Making sure we drink enough water throughout the day, ideally filtered water, can help us stay focused, energized, and emotionally balanced.

**The Benefits of a Balanced Diet:** A balanced diet is not just about eliminating certain foods but rather about incorporating various nutrient-rich foods into our daily meals. This ensures we receive all the essential vitamins and minerals our bodies need to function optimally.

<u>Here are some dietary tips to cultivate a greater sense of inner peace</u>

**Start your day with a nourishing breakfast:** A balanced breakfast, rich in protein and complex carbohydrates, provides sustained energy and helps stabilize blood sugar levels throughout the morning.

**Prioritize whole foods:** Focus on filling your plate with fruits, vegetables, whole grains, lean proteins, and healthy fats. These foods provide your body with the necessary nutrients and energy to thrive.

**Reduce processed foods and sugar:** Processed foods are often loaded with unhealthy fats, sugar, and artificial ingredients that can contribute to inflammation, mood swings, and feelings of fatigue.

**Be mindful of your eating habits:** Pay attention to your body's hunger and fullness cues. Avoid mindless snacking or eating when you're not truly hungry.

**Stay hydrated:** Drink plenty of filtered water throughout the day to stay energized and support your body's natural processes.

**Listen to your body:** Notice how different foods make you feel. If you feel sluggish or irritable after eating certain foods, consider reducing or eliminating them from your diet.

### *Embracing Food as a Tool for Peace*

By understanding the powerful connection between food and our inner state, we can use food to cultivate greater peace and well-being.

Nourishing our bodies with whole, unprocessed foods, paying attention to our blood sugar levels, supporting our gut health, staying hydrated, and practicing mindful eating habits can all contribute to greater tranquility and inner peace.

As we embark on this journey of nourishing ourselves with food, we're taking care of our physical bodies and investing in the peace of mind and emotional well-being that will ultimately lead to a more fulfilling and harmonious life.

The human body is a magnificent vessel, a complex symphony of systems working harmoniously to sustain our existence. While we often focus on the external world, neglecting the whispers of our own physical being, the truth is that true peace begins within our bodies.

Imagine your body as a garden. To nurture vibrant flowers and lush greenery, you must provide the right conditions: sunlight, water, and fertile soil. In the same way, our physical well-being plays a vital role in cultivating inner peace. Just as a neglected garden wilts and fades, so too does our inner state when we neglect the needs of our physical temple.

One of the most crucial elements of this internal garden is sleep. Sleep is not merely a period of rest but a profound, restorative process that replenishes our physical and mental resources. During sleep, our body repairs tissues, consolidates memories, and balances hormones, allowing us to wake up feeling refreshed and rejuvenated.

But sleep isn't merely about physical restoration; it's deeply intertwined with our emotional well-being. Think of your emotions as a delicate dance, and sleep as the conductor, ensuring that the rhythm of our emotions flows harmoniously. When we're sleep-deprived, our emotions become amplified and reactive. We're more likely to snap at loved ones, feel overwhelmed by everyday stressors, and succumb to negativity.

Yet, a good night's sleep is often taken for granted, dismissed as a mere luxury in our fast-paced world. We prioritize work, entertainment, and social obligations, leaving little room for the deep restorative power of sleep. We sacrifice precious hours of slumber, believing that pushing ourselves to the limit is a sign of strength. However, this relentless pursuit of productivity can lead to a chronic state of sleep deprivation, undermining our physical and mental health.

In the pursuit of inner peace, it is essential to acknowledge the importance of sleep. It's not about forcing ourselves to sleep a certain number of hours but about creating a sanctuary where our bodies can truly rest. This means prioritizing a regular sleep schedule, creating a relaxing bedtime routine, and ensuring that our sleep environment is conducive to restful sleep.

<u>Here are some practical tips for cultivating the art of sleep</u>

**Establish a Regular Sleep Schedule:**

Just like our bodies crave a consistent mealtime, they also thrive on a predictable sleep routine. Try to go to bed and wake up around the same time each day, even on weekends, to regulate your body's natural sleep-wake cycle. This helps signal to your body when it's time to wind down and when it's time to wake up.

**Create a Relaxing Bedtime Ritual:**

Before you slip into bed, create a series of calming activities that signal to your body that it's time to prepare for sleep. These could include:

1. **Warm bath:** The warmth of a bath can soothe tired muscles and calm the mind.

2. **Reading a book:** Avoid screens, but a relaxing book can help you drift off to sleep.

3. **Meditation or deep breathing exercises** can help quiet the mind and reduce racing thoughts.

4. **Gentle stretching or yoga:** Releasing tension in your body can ease your mind and promote better sleep.

5. **Listening to calming music:** Soothing music can create a tranquil atmosphere for your sleep.

**Create a Serene Sleep Environment:**

Your bedroom should be your haven, a space where you can unwind and relax. Here are a few tips for optimizing your sleep environment:

1. **Darkness:** In the dark, our bodies produce melatonin, a hormone that regulates our sleep-wake cycle. Make sure your bedroom is dark, using blackout curtains or an eye mask if necessary.

2. **Quiet:** Minimize noise distractions. Use earplugs, a white noise machine, or a fan to drown out unwanted sounds.

3. **Cool temperature:** The optimal temperature for sleep is around 65 degrees Fahrenheit.

4. **Comfortable bedding:** Invest in comfortable bedding that allows you to sleep soundly throughout the night.

**Limit Screen Time Before Bed:**

The blue light emitted from electronic devices can interfere with melatonin production, disrupting your sleep-wake cycle. Try to avoid screens for at least an hour before bed, allowing your body to prepare for rest naturally.

**Avoid Heavy Meals and Alcohol Before Bed:**

Indulging in a large meal or consuming alcohol close to bedtime can interfere with your sleep. Allow your body time to digest before going to bed.

**Get Some Sun During the Day:**

Exposure to sunlight during the day helps regulate your natural sleep-wake cycle. Try to get at least 30 minutes of sunlight each day.

**Limit Caffeine and Nicotine:**

Caffeine and nicotine are stimulants that can make it harder to fall asleep and stay asleep. Avoid these substances, especially in the afternoon and evening.

**Exercise Regularly, But Not Too Close to Bedtime:**

Regular exercise is essential for both physical and mental health, but it's best to avoid strenuous activity too close to bedtime. This can stimulate your body and make it harder to fall asleep.

**Consider a Sleep Study:**

If you're experiencing persistent sleep problems, it's wise to consult a healthcare professional. A sleep study can help identify any underlying sleep disorders that may interfere with your sleep.

Remember, sleep is not a luxury but a necessity. It's the foundation of our physical and mental well-being, allowing us to function at our best and truly experience inner peace. By prioritizing restful sleep, we're giving ourselves the gift of rejuvenation and cultivating the conditions for a calmer, more harmonious state of being.

Pursuing inner peace often involves a harmonious union between our physical and mental well-being. The body is a temple; just as we care for its physical needs, we must also tend to its emotional and mental well-being. Holistic practices, rooted in ancient wisdom, provide a pathway for cultivating this harmony.

One such practice is **yoga**, a powerful blend of physical postures, breath control, and meditation. It is more than just exercise; it is a journey of self-discovery. Yoga postures, or asanas, stretch and strengthen muscles, improving flexibility and balance. They also stimulate energy flow throughout the body, releasing tension and promoting relaxation. As we move through these postures, we learn to focus our attention on our breath, connecting with the present moment and quieting the mind. This mindful awareness extends beyond the mat, helping us approach life more easily.

**Meditation**, another ancient practice, offers a powerful tool for calming the mind and reducing stress. It involves sitting or lying in a comfortable position, focusing on the breath, and gently guiding the mind to the present moment whenever it wanders. With regular practice, meditation helps to quiet the incessant chatter of our thoughts, allowing us to access a state of deep relaxation and clarity. This sense of inner stillness extends beyond our meditation sessions, creating a more peaceful and grounded presence throughout our daily lives.

**Breathwork**, often used in conjunction with yoga and meditation, is a powerful technique for influencing our mental and emotional states. Our breath is a bridge between our physical and mental selves, and by consciously regulating our breathing, we can influence our stress levels, anxiety, and overall sense of well-being. Simple breathing exercises like deep, diaphragmatic breathing can calm the nervous system, slow the heart rate, and promote relaxation.

The practices of yoga, meditation, and breathwork are not merely about achieving physical flexibility or reducing stress. They are about connecting with the wisdom of our body and mind, learning to listen to its subtle cues, and responding with compassion and understanding.

Beyond these practices, we can cultivate a more peaceful body through **mindful movement**. This involves approaching physical activity with a focus on presence and awareness. Whether it's walking, dancing, swimming, or simply taking a stroll through nature, engage your senses, notice the sensations in your body, and appreciate the rhythm of your movement. This mindful approach transforms exercise into a practice of self-care and a gateway to inner peace.

**Nourishing our bodies with healthy foods** is vital in promoting physical and mental well-being. Eating a balanced diet rich in fruits, vegetables, whole grains, and lean protein provides the necessary nutrients for our bodies to function optimally. This, in turn, contributes to a clearer mind, a calmer nervous system, and a more peaceful state of being. Avoiding processed foods, sugary drinks, and excessive caffeine can also positively influence our mental and emotional well-being.

Finally, **prioritizing sleep and rest** is essential for maintaining physical and mental balance. Sleep allows our bodies and minds to repair, rejuvenate, and process the day's experiences. A consistent sleep schedule, a comfortable sleep environment, and a relaxing bedtime routine can contribute to a peaceful night's rest.

These holistic practices – yoga, meditation, breathwork, mindful movement, healthy eating, and restful sleep – are not separate but rather interconnected threads in the tapestry of our well-being. By incorporating them into our daily lives, we cultivate a sense of harmony within, laying the foundation for a more peaceful existence both within ourselves and in the world around us.

# 3

## THE IMPACT OF RELATIONSHIPS ON INNER PEACE

The tapestry of human life is intricately woven with the threads of relationships. These connections, whether they bring joy or sorrow, form the very fabric of our existence. Like the ebb and flow of the tides, relationships can profoundly influence our emotional state and the elusive sense of inner peace we so often yearn for.

Imagine a young woman named Amelia. She had always sought solace in the embrace of her close-knit family. Their love felt like a comforting haven, a safe space where she could be authentic without judgment. The unwavering support of her parents and siblings provided a foundation of security that helped her navigate the challenges of adolescence and young adulthood. Amelia's relationships with her loved ones cultivated a sense of belonging, a feeling of being deeply connected to something greater than herself. This deep sense of connection nurtured a tranquility within her, a sense of inner peace that emanated outward, influencing her interactions with the world.

However, life often throws unexpected curves. Amelia's idyllic world was shattered when her beloved grandmother, the matriarch of their family, succumbed to a long illness. The grief that washed over Amelia was a tempestuous storm, threatening to consume her peace. The void left by her grandmother's absence was palpable, and Amelia found herself struggling to reconcile with the reality of her loss. The once familiar comfort of her family felt strained as each member navigated their own grief in unique ways.

Amidst the turmoil, Amelia discovered a powerful truth. While her relationships had once been a source of strength and tranquility, they could also become fertile ground for conflict and turmoil. As her family grappled with their grief, unspoken resentments, and conflicting expectations surfaced. The once-solid foundation of their love felt shaky, threatened by the weight of their shared pain. Amelia realized that even amid a profound tragedy, navigating the emotional landscape with grace and understanding was crucial for maintaining inner peace.

This challenging experience taught Amelia a valuable lesson about the duality of relationships. While they can offer a sanctuary of love and support, they can also present opportunities for conflict and discord. The key, Amelia discovered, lay in recognizing the potential for both and navigating these complexities with intention. It wasn't about avoiding difficult conversations or suppressing emotions. Instead, it was about learning to communicate effectively, to listen with empathy, and to approach conflict with a desire for understanding and resolution.

Amelia's experience highlights a universal truth:

Relationships, both positive and challenging, have the power to shape our inner peace. When we cultivate healthy, supportive relationships, we create a fertile ground for inner tranquility. However, when conflicts arise or relationships become strained, they can disrupt our sense of harmony and create internal turmoil.

The journey towards inner peace through relationships is a multifaceted endeavor. It requires cultivating self-awareness, developing effective communication skills, embracing forgiveness, and practicing empathy and compassion. It requires understanding the intricate dance between our own emotional needs and the needs of those we love. It's about recognizing that each relationship, like a unique melody, adds its own harmony to the symphony of our lives.

Let's delve deeper into the impact of relationships on inner peace, exploring the intricate dance between our own emotional needs and the needs of those we love.

**The Power of Positive Relationships**

Positive relationships, like the sun's warm rays, can nourish our souls and illuminate our paths. When we surround ourselves with individuals who uplift and inspire us, we create a supportive environment that fosters our inner peace. These relationships act as a buffer against life's inevitable storms, providing a sense of belonging, validation, and security.

**A Haven of Support:** When we feel deeply connected to others, we experience a sense of belonging and being understood and accepted for who we are. This sense of belonging is a powerful antidote to loneliness and isolation, which can often lead to feelings of anxiety and depression. Supportive relationships create a haven where we can share our joys and sorrows, knowing that we are not alone in our experiences.

**A Source of Validation:** Positive relationships often offer a sense of validation, a confirmation that we are worthy and valued. Feeling loved and appreciated for who we are bolsters our self-esteem and helps us embrace our strengths and vulnerabilities. This affirmation allows us to see ourselves more clearly, fostering self-acceptance and inner peace.

**A Foundation of Security:** Secure relationships provide a sense of stability and security. Knowing that we have people in our lives who will be there for us through thick and thin provides a sense of peace and allows us to navigate challenges with greater resilience. This security creates a foundation for emotional well-being, enabling us to explore our passions, take risks, and embrace life's uncertainties.

### *The Challenge of Conflict and Discord*

While positive relationships offer a sanctuary, they can also be sources of conflict and discord. Disagreements, misunderstandings, and conflicting expectations are inevitable parts of human interaction. These challenges can create a sense of internal turmoil, disrupt our sense of peace, and leave us feeling emotionally drained.

**The Weight of Unspoken Resentments:** Conflicts often stem from unresolved issues, unspoken resentments, and unmet needs. When we fail to address these issues effectively, they fester like wounds, gradually poisoning our relationships and eroding our inner peace. Like a heavyweight, resentment can burden us with feelings of anger, bitterness, and sadness, making it difficult to experience true tranquility.

**The Strain of Unmet Expectations:** Conflicts can also arise from unmet expectations. When our perceptions of how others should act or behave don't align with their reality, it can lead to disappointment, frustration, and even resentment. These unmet expectations can create a sense of dissatisfaction and instability in our relationships, disrupting our inner peace.

**The Turmoil of Communication Breakdowns:** Effective communication is the lifeblood of healthy relationships. When communication breaks down, it can lead to misunderstandings, misinterpretations, and a spiral of conflict. This can create a sense of isolation, mistrust, and anxiety, further eroding our inner peace.

*Navigating Relationships with Intention*

The key to building peace in relationships lies in approaching them with intention. It's about understanding that relationships are a dynamic dance between our needs and those we love. It requires a willingness to communicate openly and honestly, to listen with empathy, and to approach conflict with a desire for understanding and resolution.

**The Power of Open Communication:** Open and honest communication is essential for building healthy relationships. It's about expressing our feelings and needs clearly and respectfully and actively listening to the perspectives of others. Effective communication requires a willingness to set aside our ego to approach conversations with a desire for understanding rather than winning an argument.

**The Importance of Empathy and Compassion:** Empathy is the ability to understand and share the feelings of others. When we cultivate empathy, we step into the shoes of our loved ones, trying to see the world through their eyes. This allows us to appreciate their perspectives, even if they differ from our own. Compassion, on the other hand, is the ability to feel sympathy and concern for others. When we approach our relationships with compassion, we offer kindness and understanding, even when things are difficult.

**The Transformative Power of Forgiveness:** Forgiveness is a powerful tool for releasing resentments and achieving inner peace. It's not about condoning the actions of others but about releasing ourselves from the emotional burdens of anger, bitterness, and resentment. Forgiveness sets us free from the past, allowing us to move forward with a lighter heart and a more peaceful spirit.

**The Foundation of Unconditional Love:** Unconditional love is the cornerstone of peaceful relationships. It's about accepting others for who they are, with all their imperfections, and loving them without conditions. This type of love is based on understanding, compassion, and acceptance, creating a foundation for deep connection and enduring peace.

### *Embracing the Journey of Relationships*

Relationships are integral to the human experience, offering joy and challenges. They are a constant source of growth, evolution, and transformation. By approaching our relationships with intention, cultivating effective communication, practicing empathy and compassion, and embracing forgiveness, we create a fertile ground for inner peace.

Remember, the journey to inner peace through relationships is ongoing. It requires continuous self-awareness, a willingness to learn and grow, and a commitment to building healthy, supportive connections. It's about recognizing that relationships are a symphony, each melody adding its own harmony to the grand composition of our lives. By cultivating the art of peaceful relationships, we create a tapestry of love, understanding, and enduring peace.

Finding peace within ourselves and our relationships is a profound and essential journey in a world often characterized by conflict and discord. Communication, the very fabric of human connection, is crucial in this quest for peace. Effective communication skills are not merely about conveying information; they are about building bridges of understanding, fostering empathy, and resolving differences with respect and compassion.

Imagine a garden where the soil represents our inner state, the plants our relationships, and the gardener our communication skills. The plants thrive if the soil is rich and fertile, blooming with beauty and abundance. But if the soil is neglected, the plants wither and struggle, mirroring the breakdown of trust and harmony in our relationships.

Building a peaceful garden requires nurturing the soil of our hearts through mindful and intentional communication. Let's explore some of the key principles and practices that cultivate a fertile ground for peaceful relationships:

### **Active Listening: Hearing Beyond the Words**

In the symphony of communication, active listening is the conductor, ensuring that each note and emotion is heard and understood. It's not simply about hearing the words but also paying attention to the speaker's tone of voice, body language, and unspoken nuances. It's about acknowledging the speaker's perspective, even if it differs from ours.

Imagine two friends, Emma and William, engaged in a conversation. Feeling stressed and overwhelmed, Emma expresses her frustrations about a recent work project. Instead of interrupting or offering solutions, William sits quietly, making eye contact and nodding to show he's listening. He uses verbal cues like "I see" or "Tell me more" to encourage Emma to elaborate.

Active listening creates a safe space for sharing, a haven where individuals feel heard, validated, and understood.

**<u>Empathy</u>: Stepping Into Another's Shoes**

Empathy is the bridge that connects us to another's experience. It's the ability to step into their shoes, to see the world through their eyes, and to understand their emotions, even if we disagree with them. It's about acknowledging their perspective with a compassionate heart, without judgment or dismissal.

Consider a family dinner where two siblings, Liam and Mia, argue over a shared inheritance. Feeling angry and betrayed, Liam expresses his hurt and resentment towards Mia's actions. Instead of defending herself or becoming defensive, Mia takes a deep breath and tries to understand Liam's perspective. She acknowledges his feelings, saying, "Liam, I can see how much this has hurt you, and I'm so sorry for the pain I've caused you."

Empathy, even in the face of conflict, can diffuse tension and open the door to understanding and reconciliation.

**<u>Non-Judgmental Communication</u>: The Power of Neutrality**

Judgment, like a storm cloud, can obscure the clarity of communication. It clouds our perception, hinders our understanding, and fuels conflict. Non-judgmental communication, on the other hand, creates a space for open and honest dialogue, free from bias or preconceived notions.

Picture a couple, Emily and Ethan, discussing their differing views on parenting. Ethan, advocating for stricter discipline, voices his concerns about Emily's more lenient approach. Instead of reacting defensively, Emily listens without judgment, recognizing that Ethan's concerns stem from a place of love and concern for their child. She acknowledges his perspective, saying, "Ethan, I understand your worries, and I want you to know that I'm always open to discussing this further."

Non-judgmental communication fosters mutual respect and opens the door to finding common ground.

**Constructive Feedback:** A Bridge for Growth can be a powerful personal and relational growth tool. Constructive feedback focuses on specific behaviors and their impact, offering suggestions for improvement without resorting to criticism or blame.

Imagine a colleague, David, who is struggling to meet deadlines. Instead of criticizing his performance, his manager provides constructive feedback, highlighting instances where David missed deadlines and offering suggestions for improving time management. The manager emphasizes David's strengths and expresses confidence in his ability to improve.

When offered with sincerity, constructive feedback can help individuals grow and develop, strengthening relationships and fostering collaboration.

**Expressing Needs and Boundaries:** Setting the Foundation for Peace

Setting clear boundaries is not about creating walls but about establishing healthy limits protecting our peace and wellbeing. Communicating our needs and boundaries with clarity and respect allows others to understand our limits and enables us to maintain our integrity in relationships.

Imagine a young woman, Sophia, who values her alone time.

When her friend, Emily, frequently calls her late at night, Sophia chooses to communicate her need for quiet evenings. She expresses this with kindness and empathy, saying, "Emily, I cherish our friendship and love talking to you. But I find that I need some quiet time in the evenings to recharge. Would you be open to calling me earlier in the day?"

Communicating our needs and boundaries with clarity and respect fosters understanding and helps create healthier, more peaceful relationships.

**Conflict Resolution:** A Journey of Reconciliation

Conflict is an inevitable part of human interaction. However, how we approach conflict can determine whether it leads to further division or to reconciliation and growth. Peaceful conflict resolution involves approaching disagreements with a willingness to listen, understand, and find mutually acceptable solutions.

Imagine a couple, John and Charlotte, disagreeing about their vacation plans. Instead of engaging in a shouting match, they agree to sit down and discuss their preferences openly and respectfully. They actively listen to each other's perspectives, acknowledge each other's feelings, and work together to find a compromise that meets both their needs.

Peaceful conflict resolution requires patience, empathy, and a commitment to finding common ground. It's a journey of understanding, compromise, and reconciliation.

**Forgiveness:** The Path to Liberation

Holding onto anger, resentment, or bitterness can be a heavy burden, draining our energy and hindering our inner peace. Forgiveness, the act of releasing the past, is a powerful tool for liberation. It's not about condoning hurtful actions; it's about choosing to release ourselves from the grip of negativity and pain.

Consider a young man, Daniel, who has been harboring resentment towards his father for years due to childhood abuse. He realizes that carrying this burden is only causing him pain. He decides to embark on a journey of forgiveness, seeking to release the anger and pain he's been holding onto. He understands that forgiveness doesn't necessarily mean forgetting or condoning the past; it's about freeing himself from its grip.

Forgiveness is a gift we give ourselves, a choice to break free from the chains of resentment and cultivate inner peace.

**Kindness and Compassion:** The Seeds of Peace

Kindness and compassion are the seeds of peace planted in the fertile soil of our hearts. They blossom in our words, actions, and intentions, creating a ripple effect of goodwill that extends far beyond ourselves.

Imagine a community where neighbors consistently show kindness and compassion. They help each other in need, offer encouragement, and create a sense of belonging. This shared spirit of kindness and compassion fosters a sense of unity and harmony, creating a peaceful and supportive environment.

Kindness and compassion are not just acts of charity but the foundation of a peaceful and harmonious world.

**Embracing the Imperfect:** Letting Go of Expectations

Our expectations, like rigid cages, can confine our relationships and limit our capacity for peace. They create a gap between reality and our idealized vision, leading to disappointment and frustration. Embracing the imperfect and accepting that relationships are not always perfect is a step towards cultivating peaceful acceptance.

A couple, Lisa and Henry, have been together for many years. Like all relationships, they recognize that their relationship has its challenges and imperfections. They choose to embrace this reality with acceptance and compassion, cherishing their love and working together to navigate the inevitable bumps along the way.

Embracing the imperfect allows us to see relationships for what they truly are – a tapestry of experiences, both joyful and challenging, that weave together the fabric of our lives.

**The Power of Presence:** Finding Peace in the Moment

In the whirlwind of daily life, it's easy to become consumed by the past or anxious about the future. Finding peace requires cultivating a sense of presence, being fully present in the here and now.

Imagine a group of friends gathered for a picnic. Instead of letting their minds wander to work or other responsibilities, they choose to fully engage in the present moment, savoring the taste of their food, enjoying the laughter and conversation, and appreciating the beauty of their surroundings.

Presence allows us to connect with the richness of life, appreciate the small joys, and find peace in the midst of our daily experiences.

**Building Peaceful Relationships:** A Lifelong Journey

Cultivating peaceful relationships is not a destination but a journey, a continuous process of growth and transformation. It requires ongoing commitment, self-awareness, and a willingness to learn and grow alongside our loved ones.

Like a gardener tending to their garden, we must nurture our relationships with intention, understanding, and compassion. We must cultivate the soil of our hearts, using effective communication tools to create a space for understanding, empathy, and reconciliation.

As we embrace the principles and practices outlined in this chapter, we embark on a path toward creating relationships that are not only peaceful but also fulfilling, supportive, and transformative. It's a journey of personal growth, self-discovery, and the realization that the greatest treasure we can possess is the gift of peace within ourselves and our relationships with others.

Forgiveness, a profound act of liberation, lies at the heart of building peaceful relationships. It's a journey inward, a conscious choice to release resentment, anger, and bitterness that can fester within us, poisoning our hearts and hindering our ability to experience true peace. Forgiveness isn't condoning the actions of others; it's about releasing ourselves from the shackles of the past, freeing ourselves from the heavy burden of holding onto pain.

Imagine carrying a heavy rock on your back, a constant weight that drains your energy and hinders your forward movement. This rock represents your resentment and anger, fueled by past hurts or transgressions. You might think that carrying this weight serves as a reminder of the injustice you've suffered, a way to ensure you don't repeat the same mistakes. However, the reality is that this burden only serves to perpetuate suffering, keeping you trapped in a cycle of negativity.

Forgiveness, on the other hand, is about dropping that rock. It's about releasing the pain and hurt, letting go of the need for revenge or retribution. It's about understanding that holding onto anger only harms you, not the person you are angry with.

But forgiveness isn't always easy. It requires courage and compassion, a willingness to let go of the need to be right and vindicated. It's a process, a journey that can unfold gradually, with moments of struggle and breakthroughs along the way.

The first step in forgiveness is acknowledging the pain you've experienced. This means giving voice to your emotions and allowing yourself to feel the hurt and sadness without judgment. It's about acknowledging the injustice you may have suffered but without allowing it to consume you.

The next step is to understand that you cannot change the past. Holding onto anger and resentment won't alter what has happened. It's about accepting the situation as it is, even if it's painful, and letting go of the need for things to have been different.

Once you've acknowledged the pain and accepted the past, you can begin to cultivate compassion. This means stepping into the shoes of the person who hurt you and trying to understand their perspective and motivations. It's about recognizing that everyone is struggling in their own way and that everyone is capable of making mistakes.

Forgiveness isn't about condoning the actions of the other person. It's not about forgetting what happened or minimizing the impact of the hurt. It's about releasing the anger and resentment, freeing yourself from the emotional prison you've created for yourself.

Forgiveness can be a profound act of self-love. It's about recognizing that you deserve peace and to be free from the weight of the past. It's about living in the present moment, free from the burden of past hurts.

The benefits of forgiveness extend beyond our own emotional well-being. When we forgive others, we also open the door to more peaceful and harmonious relationships. Forgiveness allows us to see people with fresh eyes, to connect with them on a deeper level, and to build bridges of understanding and compassion.

Forgiveness is a powerful tool for healing, both for ourselves and for the world around us. When we choose to forgive, we choose to break free from the chains of anger and resentment, allowing ourselves to experience the transformative power of inner peace.

Empathy and compassion are the cornerstones of peaceful relationships. They are the bridges that connect us to the hearts of others, allowing us to understand their experiences, share their joys and sorrows, and offer support in their times of need. When we cultivate empathy, we step outside our own perspective and try to see the world through the eyes of another. We open ourselves to their feelings, thoughts, and unique experiences. We listen with an open heart, seeking to understand their perspective even when it differs from ours.

Compassion, on the other hand, arises from our understanding. It is the feeling of concern and care for the well-being of others. It inspires us to offer help, comfort, and ease the suffering of those around us. When we act compassionately, we are motivated by a deep love for humanity, recognizing the interconnectedness of all beings.

In our daily lives, empathy and compassion can transform our interactions with family, friends, colleagues, and even strangers. They can soften disagreements, build bridges across divides, and foster a sense of shared humanity. Think of a time when you felt truly understood by someone. Perhaps a friend listened patiently as you confided in them, or a family member offered words of comfort during a difficult time. That feeling of being seen and heard is a powerful testament to the transformative power of empathy.

Imagine a workplace where empathy and compassion are the norm. Colleagues approach each other with understanding and a willingness to help. Conflicts are resolved through open communication and a genuine desire to find common ground. Such an environment fosters a sense of peace and enhanced productivity and creativity.

Similarly, in our communities, empathy and compassion can break down barriers of prejudice and discrimination. When we understand the experiences of those different from ourselves, we become more likely to challenge injustice and work for a more equitable world.

But empathy and compassion are not merely about feeling good about others but also about understanding ourselves. When we practice empathy, we develop a deeper self-awareness, recognizing the commonality of human emotions and experiences. We learn to be more compassionate towards our own vulnerabilities, our own mistakes, and our own struggles.

Cultivating empathy and compassion is a journey, not a destination. It requires a conscious effort to open our hearts and minds to the experiences of others. We may not always succeed, but with practice, we can learn to respond to the world with greater understanding, kindness, and love.

<u>Here are some practical steps you can take to cultivate empathy and compassion:</u>

**Practice Active Listening:** When interacting with others, make a conscious effort to truly listen to what they are saying. Pay attention to their body language, their tone of voice, and the emotions they are expressing.

**Seek Different Perspectives:** Challenge your assumptions and biases by seeking diverse viewpoints. Engage with people from different backgrounds, read about different cultures, and listen to stories that challenge your own understanding of the world.

**Consider Others' Circumstances:** When you encounter someone behaving in a difficult way, try to understand their situation. What might be contributing to their behavior? How might you respond with compassion and understanding rather than judgment?

**Practice Gratitude:** Expressing gratitude for the good in your life can help to cultivate a sense of appreciation for others. When you feel grateful for the kindness you receive, you become more likely to extend that same kindness to others.

**Engage in Acts of Kindness:** Small acts of kindness, such as offering a helping hand, expressing a compliment, or volunteering your time, can make a world of difference. When you act with kindness, you bring joy to others and cultivate empathy and compassion within yourself.

**Practice Mindfulness and Self-Compassion:** By focusing on the present moment and acknowledging your own feelings with kindness and understanding, you can cultivate a more peaceful and compassionate relationship with yourself. This, in turn, will make it easier to extend empathy and compassion to others.

By practicing these techniques, you can cultivate empathy and compassion daily, creating a more peaceful and harmonious world, beginning with yourself and extending outward to those around you.

**Love**, the most powerful force in the universe, is not merely a feeling; it's a state of being, a vibration that resonates through our very core. It's the essence of our existence, the fundamental energy that binds us to each other and the cosmos. In this section, we'll explore the transformative power of love—unconditional love, self-love, and love for others—as the bedrock of a peaceful and harmonious life.

Imagine a world where we were all connected by an invisible thread of love, an unwavering understanding that we are all part of something greater, a symphony of interconnected souls. This is the power of unconditional love, a love that transcends boundaries, judgments, and expectations. It's the love of a mother for her child, the love of a friend who supports us through thick and thin, the love that embraces us regardless of our flaws or failures. This love sets us free from the shackles of fear and insecurity, allowing us to truly connect with ourselves and others.

But before we can truly love others unconditionally, we must first cultivate self-love, the foundation upon which all other forms of love are built. Self-love is not vanity; it's the acceptance of ourselves, flaws and all. It's recognizing our inherent worth, unique gifts, and potential to contribute to the world. It's treating ourselves with the same kindness, compassion, and understanding we would extend to our loved ones.

Self-love is a journey of self-discovery, a process of peeling back the layers of doubt, fear, and negativity that have been etched onto our hearts over time. It's about embracing our imperfections, celebrating our strengths, and forgiving ourselves for our mistakes. Self-love is about silencing the inner critic that whispers doubts in our ears and replacing those negative voices with affirmations of self-worth. It's about recognizing that we deserve love, happiness, and fulfillment.

As we cultivate self-love, we open our hearts to others with greater ease and empathy. We become less reactive to the actions of others, more understanding of their struggles, and more forgiving of their mistakes. We learn to see the beauty in the imperfections of others, to appreciate their unique qualities, and to celebrate their victories.

Love for others is the natural expression of self-love. It's the ability to extend compassion, kindness, and understanding to everyone we encounter, even those who may be different from us, challenge our beliefs, or hurt us in the past. It's about recognizing the inherent worth of every human being, regardless of their background, beliefs, or behaviors.

This love is not about condoning harmful actions or ignoring injustices. It's about recognizing the shared humanity that connects us all and fostering a world where compassion and understanding prevail over judgment and anger. It's about building bridges of empathy across differences, fostering dialogue over conflict, and cultivating a sense of unity and belonging.

Here are a few simple but profound ways to cultivate love in your life:

**Practice gratitude:** Take time daily to appreciate the good things in your life, big and small. Gratitude shifts our focus from what we lack to what we have, fostering a sense of contentment and inner peace.

**Offer acts of kindness:** Do something nice for someone without expecting anything in return. Acts of kindness, even small gestures like holding a door for someone or complimenting a stranger, create ripples of positivity and strengthen our connections to others.

**Forgive yourself and others:** Holding onto resentment and anger only harms us. Forgiveness is not about condoning wrongdoing; it's about releasing ourselves from the burden of bitterness and allowing ourselves to move forward.

**Practice compassion:** Put yourself in the shoes of others and try to understand their perspectives. Compassionate understanding fosters empathy and helps us respond to others with kindness and support.

**Engage in acts of service:** Find ways to contribute to your community or the world at large. Serving others connects us to something bigger than ourselves and brings meaning to our lives.

Remember, the foundation of a peaceful and harmonious life is built upon love—unconditional love for ourselves, love for others, and love for all of life. As we cultivate these qualities within ourselves, we create a more peaceful inner world and contribute to a more peaceful and harmonious world for all.

# 4

## FINDING YOUR TRUE CALLING

Finding your true calling is like discovering a hidden treasure map within your heart. It's about aligning your actions with your deepest values and purpose, creating a sense of meaning and fulfillment that radiates outward, touching every aspect of your life. Imagine a compass pointing you toward a destination where your passions, talents, and contributions align seamlessly, creating an authentic and fulfilling life.

This journey of self-discovery is only sometimes straightforward. It often involves introspection, contemplation, and a willingness to shed limiting beliefs that may have held you back. It's about embracing your unique gifts and talents, recognizing your innate strengths, and understanding what truly lights you up from within.

Many people feel lost or unfulfilled, searching for that elusive sense of purpose. They may feel trapped in jobs that don't inspire them, relationships that drain their energy, or a routine that feels monotonous and devoid of meaning. The truth is that we all have a unique purpose to fulfill, a contribution to make to the world. This purpose is not external but an intrinsic part of our being, waiting to be unearthed.

Finding your true calling is not about finding a specific career or job; it's about aligning your life with your values and purpose. It's about living aligned with what matters most to you, making choices that resonate with your core beliefs and guiding principles. It's about recognizing the unique gifts you bring to the world and finding ways to share them with others.

There are countless stories of people who have found their true calling, transforming their lives and positively impacting the world. Consider the entrepreneur who dedicated their life to developing sustainable solutions for environmental issues, the artist who poured their soul into creating masterpieces that inspired others, or the teacher who dedicated their career to nurturing young minds and helping them reach their full potential.

These individuals, like many others, discovered their purpose and aligned their actions with their values, creating a life of profound meaning and fulfillment. They found joy in their work, a sense of purpose in their relationships, and a deep connection to something greater than themselves.

Here are some practical steps to help you embark on your journey of self-discovery:

**Reflect on your values:** What are your core beliefs and principles? What matters most to you in life? What are your non-negotiables? By understanding your values, you know what you want to stand for and how you want to live.

**Explore your interests and passions:** What activities bring you joy and fulfillment? What are you naturally good at? What subjects fascinate you? I want you to know that understanding your values leads to what ignites your enthusiasm and can offer valuable clues about your true calling.

**Identify your skills and talents:** What are you good at? What skills and abilities do you possess? Can you leverage these talents to make a positive contribution to the world?

**Connect with your intuition:** Listen to your inner voice. Pay attention to your gut feelings and those moments when you feel a strong sense of purpose or direction.

**Experiment and explore:** Be bold, try new things, step outside your comfort zone, and explore different paths. You may discover hidden talents or passions you never knew you had.

**Seek mentors and support:** Surround yourself with people who inspire you, support your dreams, and offer guidance. Their encouragement and insights can be invaluable.

**Take action:** Once you sense your purpose, bring it to life. Set small, achievable goals and celebrate your progress along the way.

<u>Here are some examples of how aligning your actions with your purpose can lead to a greater sense of meaning and peace:</u>

**A career change:** Imagine a lawyer who felt unfulfilled in their practice. They were drawn to helping people, but the legal system felt distant and cold. They decided to pursue a career in social work, where they could directly impact the lives of those in need. This change brought them immense fulfillment, a sense of purpose, and a renewed inner peace.

**A personal passion:** Imagine a musician who always loved playing the guitar but put it aside due to life's demands. They decided to dedicate time each week to playing and writing music, rekindling their passion and finding joy in expressing their creativity. This simple act brought peace and contentment they hadn't felt in years.

**A community service project:** Imagine a group of friends who felt a calling to make a difference in their community. They volunteered at a local food bank, providing meals for those experiencing hunger. This simple service gave them a sense of purpose, connection, and deep fulfillment.

Finding your true calling is not about finding a grand, life-altering purpose; it's about aligning your actions with your values and living an authentic and meaningful life. It's about discovering the unique gifts you bring to the world and sharing them with others. It's about creating a life that feels purposeful, fulfilling, and peaceful from the inside out.

The journey of self-discovery is ongoing, a continuous exploration of your values, passions, and purpose. It's about being open to new experiences, embracing challenges as opportunities for growth, and allowing yourself to be guided by your intuition and heart. As you align your life with your true purpose, you create a significant life, bringing a sense of peace and contentment that transcends external circumstances.

Pursuing our passions and making a positive contribution to the world are two powerful forces that can ignite a fire within us, leading to profound fulfillment and an unshakeable sense of inner peace. Imagine a life where you wake up each day, not simply going through the motions but fueled by a deep understanding of purpose and a burning desire to leave your mark on the world. This is the realm of passion, where our unique talents, skills, and interests converge with a calling transcending the mundane.

When we align our actions with our passions, we tap into a wellspring of energy and creativity that feels almost effortless. The hours spent pursuing our passions are not mere chores but moments of pure joy, where time seems to melt away, and we are fully present in the moment. This sense of flow, this state of being deeply engaged in something we love, is a powerful antidote to stress, boredom, and the relentless pursuit of external validation.

Furthermore, positively contributing to the world and using our gifts and talents to serve others can be profoundly transformative. It allows us to transcend the limitations of our desires and connect with something larger than ourselves. Whether volunteering at a local shelter, advocating for a cause we believe in, or simply offering a helping hand to someone in need, these acts of service not only benefit others but enrich our lives in profound ways.

By contributing to the betterment of society, we step outside of our self-centeredness and gain a broader perspective. We realize that our actions have a ripple effect, reaching far beyond ourselves and impacting the lives of others. This realization can be profoundly humbling and inspiring, leading to a sense of gratitude and a deeper appreciation for the interconnectedness of all things.

Imagine a musician composing a symphony that moves hearts and inspires minds. Or a teacher who ignites a passion for learning in the hearts of their students and shapes future generations. Or a doctor who dedicates their life to healing and alleviating suffering. These individuals are not simply pursuing their passions; they are living their purpose, making a tangible difference in the world, and, in a challenging turn, finding a sense of profound peace and fulfillment.

This journey of discovering and fulfilling our purpose is not always smooth sailing. We may encounter obstacles, setbacks, and even moments of doubt. The fear of failure, the pressure of societal expectations, and the nagging voice of self-doubt can all try to pull us away from our true calling. However, in these moments of challenge, our inner strength is tested, and our resilience is forged.

The path to fulfilling our purpose is not about achieving perfection but embracing the journey, with all its triumphs and tribulations. It's about learning from our mistakes, celebrating our successes, and continuously striving to grow and evolve.

Here are some practical steps you can take to discover your passions and make a positive contribution to the world:

1. **Explore your interests:** Take some time to reflect on the activities that bring you joy, spark your curiosity, and make you feel truly alive. What are you naturally good at? What makes you lose track of time? What topics could you talk about for hours?

2. **Identify your values:** What are the core principles that guide your life? What is important to you? What kind of impact do you want to make on the world? By understanding your values, you can start to align your actions with your beliefs.

3. **Seek inspiration:** Surround yourself with people and stories that inspire you. Read books, watch films, and listen to podcasts featuring individuals living their purpose and making a difference.

4. **Take small steps:** It's easy to get overwhelmed when discovering your purpose. Start by taking small, manageable steps instead of figuring everything out at once. Try a new activity, volunteer, or connect with someone who shares

your interests.

5. **Don't be afraid to experiment:** The path to purpose is often winding. It may require experimentation and a willingness to try new things. Embrace the journey of exploration and discovery, and don't be afraid to make mistakes.

6. **Embrace gratitude:** Take time each day to appreciate the good things in your life. By focusing on gratitude, you shift your perspective from lack to abundance and cultivate a more positive mindset.

7. **Find your tribe:** Connect with others who share your passions and values. Surround yourself with people who support your dreams and inspire you to live a life of purpose.

The journey of discovering our passions and positively contributing to the world is deeply personal. It's not about achieving a predefined level of success or accolades. It's about aligning our lives with our values, following our inner compass, and making a difference in the world in a way that feels authentic and meaningful. And in doing so, we unlock a profound sense of fulfillment, peace, and purpose that transcends the limitations of material wealth and external validation.

Fear and doubt, like shadows lurking in the corners of our minds, can cast a long and daunting presence over our lives. They whisper insidious lies, telling us we're not good, capable, or worthy enough to pursue our dreams and live our purpose. These limiting beliefs, deeply ingrained within us through years of conditioning, can act as invisible chains, holding us back from realizing our full potential and finding true fulfillment.

But what if these shadows were merely illusions, fleeting and temporary? What if we had the power to step into the light, break free from their grip, and embrace the boundless possibilities that lie within us?

Fear and doubt are not our masters; they are simply reactions and ingrained patterns of thought that can be challenged and transformed. Overcoming these internal obstacles is not about eradicating them completely but about understanding their origins, learning to recognize them for what they are, and developing the resilience to navigate their whispers without letting them dictate our lives.

Imagine a ship sailing across the vast ocean, guided by a compass pointing towards a distant horizon. The journey has its challenges - stormy seas, unpredictable currents, and the occasional fog that obscures the path. But the ship's captain, armed with experience, knowledge, and unwavering determination, steers the vessel through each obstacle, using the compass to guide its course.

We are the captains in our lives, and our purpose is the compass. Fear and doubt are the storms, the currents, and the fog we encounter along the way. We can succumb to their power, allowing them to pull us off course. Alternatively, we can embrace our inner strength, courageously navigate their challenges, and continue sailing toward our ultimate destination.

Here are a few practical strategies to overcome fear and doubt, unlock the power within us, and embrace the life we were meant to live:

**Identify and Challenge Limiting Beliefs:**

The first step in overcoming fear and doubt is to understand their roots. These limiting beliefs are often deeply ingrained, stemming from childhood experiences, societal conditioning, or past failures. Identifying these beliefs is crucial to beginning the process of transformation.

Imagine you're a sculptor working with a block of marble.

Your vision is clear, but the marble must be refined and unrefined. Before you can carve your masterpiece, you must first identify the imperfections and flaws in the stone.

Similarly, we must first identify the negative beliefs that hold us back to overcome fear and doubt. Ask yourself questions like:

What limiting beliefs are holding me back from pursuing my purpose?

Where did these beliefs originate?

What evidence supports or contradicts these beliefs?

Once you've identified these limiting beliefs, you can challenge them with a spirit of inquiry and critical thinking. Ask yourself:

Are these beliefs indeed true, or are they simply assumptions?

What evidence exists to support or refute these beliefs? How do these beliefs affect my actions, choices, and overall well-being?

By consciously examining and challenging these beliefs, you dismantle their power over your mind and open yourself to new possibilities.

**Embrace Vulnerability and Seek Support:**

Overcoming fear and doubt is not a solitary journey. It requires vulnerability and a willingness to seek support from others who understand and empathize with our struggles.

Imagine a hiker scaling a mountain, facing steep inclines, rocky paths, and treacherous weather. While the hiker possesses the strength and skill to navigate the terrain, they are also aware of their limitations. They know that relying on their strength alone is not enough; they need the support and guidance of experienced climbers and experienced companions who can help them overcome obstacles and stay on course.

Similarly, in our journeys, we can't afford to be afraid of vulnerability or shy away from support. Connecting with trusted friends, mentors, or support groups can provide a safe space to share our fears, doubts, and insecurities, to receive encouragement, and to learn from others who have overcome similar challenges.

**Practice Mindfulness and Self-Compassion:**

Mindfulness, the practice of bringing our attention to the present moment without judgment, is a powerful tool for overcoming fear and doubt. When mindful, we become aware of our thoughts and emotions without getting swept away.

Imagine a river flowing steadily towards the sea. Its waters are sometimes calm and serene, sometimes turbulent and forceful. Yet, the river continues flowing, adapting to the changing currents and obstacles it encounters.

In the same way, our minds are constantly flowing with thoughts and emotions. Some are positive and uplifting, while others are negative and distressing. Mindfulness lets us observe these currents without getting caught up in their intensity. Practicing mindfulness, we learn to identify and acknowledge our fears and doubts without allowing them to control our actions.

Self-compassion, the ability to treat ourselves with kindness, understanding, and acceptance, is also essential for overcoming fear and doubt. When we are self-compassionate, we recognize that everyone experiences fear and doubt, and we treat ourselves with the same empathy and understanding we would offer a dear friend.

**Cultivate Gratitude and Appreciation:**

Gratitude, acknowledging and appreciating the good in our lives, is a powerful antidote to fear and doubt. When we focus on what we are grateful for, our perspective shifts from lack to abundance, and our minds become more open to possibilities.

Imagine a farmer who tends to a field of flowers. They are grateful for the fertile soil, the gentle sunlight, and the refreshing rain that nourishes their plants. They appreciate the beauty of the flowers, the vibrant colors, and the delicate fragrance they emit.

Similarly, when we cultivate gratitude, we appreciate the beauty and abundance in our lives. We acknowledge the love and support we receive from others, our unique gifts and talents, and the challenges we have overcome. Gratitude shifts our focus from what we lack to what we have, creating a sense of contentment and inner peace.

**Take Action and Embrace Imperfection:**

Overcoming fear and doubt often requires action, even when uncertain or apprehensive. We build momentum and gain confidence in our abilities by taking small, deliberate steps toward our goals.

Imagine a musician learning to play a new instrument. At first, their fingers fumble, their notes could be more cohesive, and their progress could be faster. Yet, they persevere, practicing diligently, gradually improving their skills, and developing their talent.

Similarly, in our journeys, we must be willing to take action, even when unsure or afraid. By embracing imperfection and learning from our mistakes, we build resilience and grow in confidence. Every step we take and every challenge we overcome brings us closer to realizing our purpose and finding fulfillment.

**Visualize Your Success and Embrace Positive Affirmations:**

Visualization, creating vivid mental images of our desired outcomes, is a powerful tool for reprogramming our minds and cultivating a belief in our abilities. When we visualize ourselves succeeding, we activate the power of our subconscious mind, aligning our thoughts and actions with our goals.

Imagine a painter standing before a blank canvas, their mind filled with a vision of a magnificent landscape. They see the rolling hills, the sparkling river, and the majestic mountains in their mind's eye. They bring their vision to life on the canvas with each brush stroke.

Similarly, when we visualize our success, we create a blueprint for our future. We see ourselves achieving our goals, overcoming challenges, and experiencing the joy of fulfillment. By visualizing our dreams with clarity and conviction, we plant seeds of possibility in our subconscious minds, paving the way for their manifestation in the real world.

Positive affirmations are powerful statements that reinforce our desired beliefs and outcomes. They remind us of our strength, worthiness, and ability to achieve our goals. By repeating these affirmations regularly, we begin to reprogram our subconscious mind, replacing negative beliefs with positive ones.

Imagine a gardener nurturing a delicate flower. They speak words of encouragement, assuring the plant of its strength, its beauty, and its ability to thrive. They gently water the soil, providing the nourishment it needs to flourish.

Similarly, when we use positive affirmations, we nurture our inner strength and potential. We affirm and encourage ourselves, reminding us of our worthiness, abilities, and capacity to create the life we desire.

**Find Your Tribe and Celebrate Your Wins:**

Surrounding yourself with supportive and inspiring individuals who believe in your dreams can make a difference in overcoming fear and doubt. When you have a community that celebrates your wins, offers encouragement during setbacks, and holds you accountable for your goals, you're more likely to persevere through challenges and reach your full potential.

Imagine a team of athletes training for a significant competition. They push themselves to their limits, knowing that their success depends not only on their efforts but also on the strength and support of their teammates. They celebrate each other's victories, offer encouragement during setbacks, and work together to achieve their common goal.

Similarly, in our journeys, we need a tribe of supporters who believe in our dreams and encourage us to strive for greatness. We need friends, mentors, and fellow travelers who can celebrate our wins, offer a listening ear during setbacks, and hold us accountable for our goals.

**Practice Patience and Embrace the Process:**

Overcoming fear and doubt is not a linear process. It's a journey that requires patience, persistence, and a willingness to embrace the ups and downs. There will be moments of progress and moments of setback, times when we feel strong and times when we feel vulnerable.

Imagine a sculptor who has devoted countless hours to crafting a masterpiece. They work meticulously, chiseling away at the stone, refining their design with each stroke. There will be moments when they feel satisfied with their progress and when they struggle with the complexity of their vision. Yet, they remain committed to their craft, trusting in the process and knowing that the final product will be worth the effort.

Similarly, in our journeys, we must be patient and persistent. We must embrace the growth process, recognizing that setbacks are not failures but opportunities to learn, adapt, and refine our approach.

Overcoming fear and doubt is not about erasing them but learning to navigate their whispers without letting them dictate our lives. It's about embracing vulnerability, seeking support, practicing mindfulness and self-compassion, cultivating gratitude and appreciation, taking action, embracing imperfection, visualizing our success, using positive affirmations, finding our tribe, and embracing the process.

By implementing these strategies, we can begin to dismantle the limitations we have imposed upon ourselves, unlock the boundless potential within, and embrace the life we were meant to live. The journey may not always be easy, but with courage, determination, and a willingness to learn and grow, we can overcome any obstacle and create a life filled with purpose, fulfillment, and lasting peace.

**Gratitude** is a powerful catalyst for transformation, a beacon of light that shines through the darkness of negativity. It's the antidote to a life fixated on what we lack, replacing it with a profound appreciation for the abundance surrounding us. When we cultivate gratitude, we shift our focus from the scarcity of our perceived limitations to the richness of the blessings in our lives.

Imagine a simple act like waking up in the morning. For many, it's a moment filled with rush and worry. But what if we paused for a moment, genuinely allowing ourselves to appreciate the gift of another day? The warmth of the sun on our skin, the fresh air filling our lungs, the ability to move our bodies, and the fact that we're alive are all things we take for granted, yet they represent a wellspring of gratitude.

Gratitude is not just about expressing thankfulness; it's about cultivating a mindset of appreciation. It's about noticing the small joys that often get overlooked, the beauty in the mundane, and the kindness surrounding us. A warm smile from a stranger, a heartfelt hug from a loved one, and a moment of calm in the midst of chaos are all opportunities to practice gratitude.

The act of gratitude profoundly impacts our mental and emotional well-being. We create a space for contentment when we shift our focus from what we lack to what we have. Contentment is not about settling for less or becoming complacent; it's about finding peace and happiness within ourselves, regardless of our external circumstances.

Gratitude can transform our inner landscape, replacing negativity with positivity, anxiety with serenity, and doubt with belief. It's a tool that empowers us to navigate life's challenges with greater resilience and a sense of inner peace.

The key to unlocking the transformative power of gratitude is to make it a conscious practice. We can begin by cultivating a daily ritual of appreciation. Please take a few moments each morning to reflect on everything we're grateful for. Start small: a warm bed, a cup of coffee, the sound of birdsong. As we expand our awareness, we notice the abundance surrounding us.

Gratitude can also be practiced throughout the day. When we feel stressed or overwhelmed, we can shift our focus by taking a moment to appreciate something simple. The coolness of a breeze, the taste of a delicious meal, and the warmth of a sunny day are all opportunities to cultivate gratitude and create a sense of peace.

Gratitude is not just a feeling; it's an act. We can express our appreciation through words, actions, and even small gestures. A simple "thank you" can go a long way in creating a positive ripple effect. We can also express gratitude through acts of kindness, helping someone in need, or performing random acts of generosity.

By cultivating a life of gratitude, we open ourselves to the abundance surrounding us, transforming our experiences from lack to abundance, negativity to positivity, and stress to serenity. Gratitude is not just a practice; it's a way of life, a mindset that creates a foundation for peace, fulfillment, and joy.

Imagine a world where gratitude was the currency of human interaction, acts of kindness were the norm, and the pursuit of happiness was rooted in the appreciation of the present moment. This is the world that gratitude can create for us and the world around us. It's a world where peace is not a distant dream but a lived reality, a tapestry woven with threads of thankfulness, appreciation, and love.

We all have the power to cultivate gratitude. It's a simple yet profound practice that can transform our lives, one grateful thought, one kind act, one peaceful moment at a time. Let us embrace the transformative power of gratitude and create a world filled with peace, joy, and abundance.

Living a life aligned with your purpose is like navigating a ship across a vast ocean. Your purpose is your compass, guiding you toward a destination of fulfillment and meaning. The journey is aligning your values, beliefs, and actions with this inner compass.

Here's how you can chart your course toward a life of purpose and peace:

**Know Yourself:** The first step is understanding who you are, what you deeply value, and what brings you joy.

Please just reflect on your passions, interests, talents, and skills. Journaling, meditation, and time in nature can help you connect with your inner self and uncover your true purpose.

**Define Your Purpose:** Once you understand your values and passions, begin to shape your purpose. It's not about finding a grand, life-altering mission but a meaningful direction for your life. Your purpose can be a simple yet powerful statement, like "To live a life of love and service" or "To create art that inspires joy."

**Take Inspired Action:** Once you understand your purpose, start taking small, inspired actions towards it. Take your time with grand plans. Focus on taking one step at a time. If you want to be a writer, write for 15 minutes daily. If you want to help others, volunteer at a local soup kitchen. Each action, no matter how small, contributes to the larger goal of aligning your life with your purpose.

**Embrace the Flow:** As you move forward, be open to the unexpected twists and turns that life throws. Sometimes, the path toward your purpose may need to be more transparent and more straightforward than expected. Trust your intuition and embrace the flow of life. Flexibility and adaptability are essential for navigating the journey with grace.

**Celebrate Your Progress:** Acknowledge and celebrate your achievements along the way. Recognize the small wins and milestones. Celebrate the courage to step outside your comfort zone and move towards your purpose. Appreciation and gratitude will fuel your motivation and keep you moving forward.

**Seek Guidance:** Be bold and seek guidance from mentors, coaches, or spiritual advisors. They can provide support, encouragement, and valuable insights as you navigate your journey. Sharing your aspirations with others can foster accountability and a sense of community.

**Embrace the Unknown:** The journey towards living a life of purpose is not about reaching a destination but embracing life's continuous unfolding. There will be times of uncertainty, doubt, and even fear. But in those moments, you can learn, grow, and discover even more about yourself and your purpose.

**Finding Your Purpose Through Service:** A powerful way to connect with your purpose is to serve others. This could take many forms, such as volunteering at a local charity, mentoring a young person, or simply offering a kind word to someone in need. We step outside of ourselves by serving others and connecting with something larger than ourselves. This act of giving can bring a deep sense of fulfillment and peace.

**Discovering Your Passion:** Passion is the fuel that ignites our purpose. What are you passionate about? What activities make you lose track of time? What brings you joy and a sense of aliveness? Once you identify your passions, explore ways to integrate them into your life. You can turn a hobby into a side hustle or find a career that aligns with your passions.

**Overcoming Limiting Beliefs:** Many of us hold limiting beliefs that prevent us from living our purpose. These beliefs may stem from past experiences, societal conditioning, or fears. Become aware of these beliefs and challenge them. Ask yourself, "What if this belief isn't true?" "What would I do if I didn't have this belief?" By confronting these limiting beliefs, you can open yourself up to new possibilities and live a more authentic and fulfilling life.

**The Power of Gratitude:** Gratitude is a powerful tool for cultivating peace and joy. When we focus on the good in our lives, we shift our attention away from lack and scarcity. Practice gratitude by keeping a gratitude journal and writing down things you are grateful for daily. Express gratitude to the people in your life, and appreciate the beauty surrounding you.

Living a life of purpose and peace is an ongoing journey of self-discovery, aligning your actions with your values, and embracing the flow of life. It is a journey of heart and spirit, where you learn to trust your intuition, overcome limiting beliefs, and discover the immense power within you. It is a journey worth taking.

# 5

## THE NATURE OF ATTACHMENT

Imagine a world where your heart feels light, unburdened by the weight of anxieties and fears. Imagine a life where every moment is met with a sense of calm, even amidst the turbulence of life's storms. This is the world of inner peace – a state of being that transcends the fleeting happiness offered by external factors and resides in the depths of our being. Yet, attaining this sanctuary of inner peace often requires us to confront and let go of the very things we hold dear: our attachments.

In their essence, attachments are the threads that bind us to the external world – a world of constant change, uncertainty, and impermanence. These threads can be woven from material possessions, people we love, desired outcomes, or specific beliefs and ideas. They can be subtle, like a gentle tug on our heartstrings, or solid and forceful, creating a vise-like grip on our happiness.

Imagine a man who finds his identity and self-worth solely in his impressive career. He dedicates himself to climbing the corporate ladder, sacrificing his time, energy, and even personal relationships to pursue success. His life revolves around achieving a specific outcome – a promotion, a raise, a coveted title. Thoughts of his career consume every moment, his mind constantly racing, planning, and strategizing. This man has become attached to the idea of success and the external validation it brings. This attachment fuels his anxiety, fear of failure, and an insatiable desire for more. His inner peace is perpetually elusive, hostage to the ever-shifting tides of the corporate world.

In the same way, consider a woman who finds her happiness solely in the approval of others. She spends countless hours curating her online persona, striving to present a flawless image that attracts likes and admiration. Her self-worth is contingent on the number of followers, the comments she receives, and the validation she gains from the virtual world. This woman has become attached to the external validation of others, to the illusion of acceptance and love that comes from the superficiality of social media. This attachment leads to insecurity, inadequacy, and a constant need for external validation. Her true self, her authentic voice, remains hidden behind a carefully constructed facade, hindering her ability to find true inner peace.

Attachments to material possessions can also create a sense of unease and anxiety. Imagine a family that accumulates vast wealth, meticulously accumulating designer clothes, luxury cars, and extravagant homes. They believe their happiness lies in owning these material possessions and maintaining a certain level of external wealth and status. Yet, as they acquire more, they find themselves consumed by a gnawing fear of loss. They become obsessed with protecting their possessions, constantly worried about theft, damage, or the potential for financial decline. This attachment to material possessions becomes a source of stress, anxiety, and a feeling of constant insecurity, preventing them from truly experiencing the serenity of inner peace.

The key to releasing these attachments and reclaiming our inner peace lies in understanding the nature of impermanence. The world around us is constantly in flux – possessions can be lost, relationships can change, and outcomes may not always align with our expectations. When we attach ourselves to these impermanent things, we set ourselves up for disappointment and suffering. Whenever these attachments are challenged or threatened, our inner peace is shaken, replaced by fear, anxiety, and a sense of being out of control.

Furthermore, attachments create an illusion of control. They feed the illusion that we can hold onto things, people, or outcomes and that by doing so, we can ensure our happiness. However, the reality is that we have no control over the external world. We cannot force people to behave in a certain way, we cannot guarantee that our material possessions will always remain, and we cannot control the outcome of every event. This illusion of control, born out of our attachments, creates tension, fear, and anxiety, robbing us of the tranquility of accepting life.

# THE CURRENCY OF PEACE

The path to inner peace is paved with the willingness to let go. It is a conscious choice to detach ourselves from the external world and find solace in the depths of our being. This journey of letting go is not about abandoning the people or things we love but rather about recognizing that true happiness lies within ourselves, not in the external world.

It is about cultivating a sense of acceptance, acknowledging that things change, people change, and outcomes are not always within our control. It is about finding contentment in the present moment and appreciating the beauty and simplicity of life without the need for external validation or rewards.

The journey to letting go can be challenging. It requires courage to confront our attachments and to acknowledge the fears that keep us clinging to them. It requires patience as we navigate the emotional roller coaster of releasing these ties. It requires practice as we learn to shift our focus from the external to the internal, from the fleeting to the enduring.

Next, we will explore the transformative power of acceptance. We will delve into the profound wisdom of embracing things as they are, letting go of resistance, and discovering the liberation that comes from surrendering to the flow of life.

Acceptance is the key that unlocks the door to inner peace. It's the art of relinquishing our resistance to what is, allowing us to navigate the ebb and flow of life with grace and poise. When we embrace acceptance, we step out of the constant struggle to control and force things to be different. Instead, we choose to embrace the present moment, imperfections, and all.

Think of it as a wave crashing against a rocky shore. The wave, fueled by the tide, has immense power and energy. If the shore resists and holds onto its rigid form, the wave will crash against it, creating a chaotic, destructive force. But if the shore accepts the wave and surrenders to its power, the wave will flow over it, leaving a gentle ripple and a sense of calm.

We are like that shore. The events of our lives, challenges, disappointments, and uncertainties are like the waves. They are forces beyond our control. When we resist them, when we try to fight them, we create inner turmoil, anxiety, and suffering. But when we accept them and acknowledge their presence without judgment or resistance, we allow them to flow through us, leaving a sense of tranquility and peace.

Acceptance doesn't mean resignation or apathy. It doesn't mean giving up on our dreams or aspirations. It simply means understanding that we don't have control over everything. We can't force things to be different. We can only sometimes get what we want. And sometimes, we must accept that there are things in life that we cannot change.

This doesn't mean we passively accept everything that comes our way. Acceptance is not about complacency. It's about embracing the reality of the situation and understanding that we have the power to respond to it rather than the power to control it.

For example, let's say you've been working hard towards a specific goal, a promotion, a big project, or a life-changing decision. You've put in all the effort and given it your all, but it still doesn't work out the way you expected. You feel disappointed, frustrated, maybe even angry.

Instead of resisting the outcome and trying to force things to change, acceptance invites you to acknowledge your feelings and allow yourself to feel the disappointment without judgment. It encourages you to step back, take a breath, and ask yourself "What can I learn from this experience? What can I do differently next time?"

Acceptance isn't about giving up. It's about letting go of the need to control and be in charge of every detail. It's about understanding that life is a journey; sometimes, our path must reach our envisioned destination. But the trip was with purpose.

Acceptance allows us to see the beauty and meaning in every moment, even the difficult ones. It helps us appreciate the lessons learned, the wisdom gained, and the growth that emerges from adversity.

Acceptance also involves releasing the need for things to be perfect. We live in a world of ideals, "should, " and "ought's." We strive for perfection, but in doing so, we often miss out on the simple joys and beauty of the present moment.

Acceptance encourages us to embrace the imperfections, to see the beauty in the flaws, the humor in the mistakes, and the resilience in the struggles. It reminds us that life is not about achieving some ultimate goal but about savoring the journey, embracing the ups and downs, and appreciating the richness and complexity of it all.

Here's how acceptance can work in practice:

1. **Observe Your Thoughts:** Please pay attention to your thoughts, especially those that are harmful, resistant, or controlling. Notice the patterns, the recurring themes, and the phrases you use.

2. **Challenge Your Beliefs:** Question your assumptions about how things should be. Are your expectations realistic? Are you clinging to a specific outcome that may not be the best for you?

3. **Acknowledge Your Feelings:** Don't try to suppress or ignore your emotions. Allow yourself to feel the disappointment, the frustration, the anger, the sadness. Permit yourself to feel.

4. **Practice Gratitude:** Focus on what you have, not what you lack. Cultivate a sense of appreciation for the good things in your life, the people you love, the experiences you've had, and the lessons you've learned.

5. **Embrace the Present Moment:** Practice mindfulness,

bringing your attention to the here-and-now sensations in your body, the sounds around you, and the thoughts that arise in your mind.

6. **Let Go of Control:** Release the need to control everything. Understand that some things are simply beyond your influence. Focus your energy on what you can control: your reactions, choices, and actions.

7. **Practice Acceptance Rituals:** Find ways to incorporate acceptance into your daily routine. It could be a simple act of gratitude, a mindful breathing exercise, quiet reflection, or a conscious decision to embrace the present moment.

8. **Be Kind to Yourself:** Acceptance is a journey, not a destination. There will be times when you struggle, when you resist, and when you feel overwhelmed. That's okay. Be patient, learn from your mistakes, and keep moving forward.

Acceptance is a powerful tool for creating inner peace and harmony. It's a journey that requires practice, patience, and self-compassion. But the rewards are worth the effort. By embracing acceptance, we release ourselves from the shackles of control, embrace the present moment's reality, and unlock the door to a life filled with tranquility, joy, and a deep sense of inner peace.

Fear and anxiety can be formidable obstacles on the path to peace. They are often rooted in our past experiences, worries about the future, or perceptions of the present moment. These feelings can hijack our thoughts, consume our energy, and prevent us from fully experiencing life's joy and tranquility. But the good news is that fear and anxiety are not our masters. We can cultivate resilience and navigate these emotions with grace and composure.

One of the most fundamental ways to manage fear and anxiety is through the practice of deep breathing. When we feel overwhelmed, our breath becomes shallow and rapid, feeding the cycle of stress and tension. However, Deep, conscious breathing can help calm our nervous system and bring us back to a state of balance. Techniques such as diaphragmatic, box, and alternate nostril breathing can help regulate our heart rate, lower blood pressure, and ease feelings of panic. These simple yet powerful exercises directly connect to our physical body, grounding us in the present moment and allowing us to regain control.

Meditation is another potent practice for releasing fear and anxiety. It involves focusing on a single point, whether our breath, a mantra, or a specific object. As we sit in quiet contemplation, we detach from the constant flow of thoughts and emotions that often fuel our worries. Meditation allows us to cultivate mindfulness, observing our thoughts and feelings without judgment. This non-judgmental awareness enables us to step back from the grip of fear and anxiety, allowing us to experience a sense of peace and clarity.

Positive affirmations are a powerful tool for reprogramming our subconscious mind. When we repeat positive statements about ourselves, our abilities, and our future, we shift our beliefs and create a more positive self-image. Affirmations can help to counter the negative self-talk that often fuels fear and anxiety. They remind us of our strength, resilience, and capacity for joy.

Imagine, for example, someone battling a fear of public speaking. They might use affirmations such as "I am confident and articulate. My voice is strong and clear. I enjoy sharing my ideas with others." By repeating these affirmations regularly, they can gradually rewire their subconscious mind, reducing their fear and increasing their confidence.

While deep breathing, meditation, and affirmations are excellent tools for managing fear and anxiety, it's essential to acknowledge that sometimes, we need additional support. Talking to a therapist or counselor can be incredibly helpful in addressing underlying issues that contribute to our fears. They can provide a safe and non-judgmental space to explore our anxieties, develop coping strategies, and challenge negative thought patterns.

It's also crucial to remember that fear and anxiety are not necessarily signs of weakness. They are natural human emotions that serve a purpose. Fear can protect us from danger, and anxiety can motivate us to take action. However, when these emotions become overwhelming or debilitating, we must learn to manage them effectively.

By practicing deep breathing, meditation, and positive affirmations, we can equip ourselves with the tools to navigate fear and anxiety with greater resilience and peace.

It's a journey of self-discovery and empowerment, allowing us to reclaim our inner peace and live a life filled with joy, purpose, and fulfillment.

The concept of surrender often needs to be understood. It's not about giving up or becoming passive, but rather a conscious choice to release control and trust in a force greater than ourselves. It's about letting go of the need to micromanage our lives and embracing the flow of life with an open heart. This surrender can be liberating and transformative, creating profound peace and freedom.

Imagine a river, a powerful current flowing with unwavering momentum. Trying to fight against the river's current, to swim upstream, would be exhausting and ultimately futile. Instead, a wise traveler would recognize the wisdom of surrendering to the flow. They would float with the current, navigating the twists and turns, trusting that the river would lead them to their destination.

In the context of our spiritual journey, surrender is about aligning ourselves with this natural flow of life. It's about recognizing that we are not in control of everything and that greater intelligence is at play, guiding us toward our highest good. This force, this higher power, can be understood as the universe, a divine presence, or simply the natural order of things.

Surrendering to this higher power requires letting go of our ego's need to control, plan, predict, and be in charge. It's about trusting that we are exactly where we need to be, even when things don't go as planned. This means we become active and aware of precisely our responsibilities. It means we act with intention but without attachment to specific outcomes. We trust that whatever happens is for our benefit, even if it doesn't make sense now.

Surrender is a practice, a conscious choice that requires ongoing attention and commitment. It's about developing a deep faith in the unfolding of life, a trust that things are working out exactly as they should, even when our minds struggle to comprehend it.

There are many ways to cultivate the practice of surrender.

<u>Here are a few suggestions:</u>

**Meditation:** Regular meditation can help us quiet the mind, connect with our inner wisdom, and develop a more profound sense of trust. Through meditation, we can observe our thoughts and emotions without judgment, allowing them to come and go without clinging to them. This creates space for us to surrender to the present moment and the unfolding of life.

**Prayer:** Whether religious or spiritual, prayer can be a powerful tool for surrendering to a higher power. By pouring out our anxieties, fears, and desires, we acknowledge that we are not in control and that there is a force greater than ourselves to whom we can turn. Prayer can help us connect with a source of strength, guidance, and peace.

**Affirmations:** Positive affirmations, such as "I surrender to the divine plan" or "I trust in the flow of life," can help reprogram our subconscious minds to embrace surrender. By repeating these affirmations regularly, we are planting seeds of faith and trust, strengthening our ability to let go.

**Gratitude:** A gratitude practice can help us shift our focus from what we lack to what we have. When we are grateful, we are acknowledging the abundance in our lives, the blessings that surround us, and the guidance that is always present. This gratitude can help us let go of our need to control and embrace the present moment.

**Acceptance:** The practice of acceptance is crucial to surrender. It's about accepting things as they are, even when challenging. It's about letting go of resistance and simply allowing ourselves to be present with our experiences. Acceptance doesn't mean approval or condoning; instead, it means recognizing reality without judgment.

Surrender is not a passive act but an active choice. It's about recognizing that true power lies not in control but in the willingness to let go. When we surrender, we open ourselves to more profound peace, joy, and connection. We trust the wisdom of the universe, the guiding force that knows what's best for us, even when we can't see it.

As we surrender, we may find that our anxieties and fears begin to dissolve. We may experience a sense of lightness, freedom, and contentment. We may even discover a new strength, a resilience that arises from trusting in something greater than ourselves.

Surrendering is not an easy practice, but it is profoundly rewarding. It's about releasing the need to control and embracing the flow of life with an open heart. It's about trusting in the universe's wisdom and allowing ourselves to be guided toward our highest good. We unlock a deeper level of peace, freedom, and fulfillment as we surrender.

Imagine a world where your heart is a sanctuary, a calm place amidst the chaos. Imagine a life where you navigate the ups and downs with unwavering inner peace. This freedom awaits you when you learn the art of letting go.

Letting go isn't about surrendering to the whims of fate or becoming apathetic. It's about freeing yourself from the chains of attachment and fear, allowing yourself to be fully present in each moment without the weight of expectations or the grip of anxieties.

## Detachment: The Art of Non-Attachment

Imagine a beautiful flower, its petals unfurling gracefully in the sun. It doesn't cling to the warmth or fear the coming night. It simply blooms, offering its beauty to the world without holding on. This is the essence of detachment.

**Material Possessions:** Think about the things you own. Do you hold on to them tightly, fearing loss? Or can you appreciate their value without being attached to their possession? Detachment with material possessions isn't about becoming a minimalist but finding a balance between appreciation and non-attachment.

**Relationships:** This can be one of the most challenging areas for letting go. We often attach ourselves to how relationships should be or how we think they should make us feel. This can lead to disappointment and heartbreak when reality doesn't meet our expectations. Instead, let go of the need to control others or the outcome of relationships. Embrace the beauty of connection while understanding that people change and relationships evolve.

**Outcomes:** We often hold onto expectations about how things should turn out. This can create unnecessary stress and anxiety. Imagine a surfer riding a wave. He doesn't control the wave; he surfs it with skill and grace. In the same way, let go of the need to control the outcome of events in your life. Accept what is, and embrace the journey.

### *Confronting Your Fears*

Fear is a natural human emotion, but it can paralyze us if we let it. Many of our fears are based on imagined scenarios or past experiences that we cling to.

**Identifying Your Fears:** The first step is to recognize your fears. What are you afraid of? Losing your job? Public speaking? Once you acknowledge your fears, you can begin to address them.

**Challenging Your Fears:** Ask yourself, "What is the worst thing that could happen?" Is it truly as terrible as you imagine? Most often, our fears are exaggerated.

**Taking Action:** Sometimes, facing it head-on is the best way to overcome fear. If you need more confidence in public speaking, start by speaking in front of small groups. If you're afraid of heights, take a small step onto a ladder. Each small step helps build confidence and diminish fear.

### *The Practice of Letting Go*

Letting go is a continuous process, not a one-time event. It requires practice and patience. Here are some techniques to cultivate the art of letting go:

**Mindfulness:** Pay attention to your thoughts and feelings without judgment. Notice when you're holding onto an attachment or fear. Observe it without getting caught up in it.

**Meditation:** Meditation is a powerful tool for quieting the mind and letting go of thoughts and emotions. Even a few minutes of daily meditation can make a significant difference.

**Journaling:** Write about your fears, attachments, and experiences of letting go. Journaling allows you to process your thoughts and emotions, releasing them from your mind.

**Gratitude:** Focus on the good things in your life, no matter how small. Gratitude shifts your focus from what you lack to what you have, fostering a sense of contentment and letting go of the need for more.

**Acceptance:** Embrace the present moment's reality without trying to change it. Accept that you can't control everything in your life, and let go of the need to resist what is.

### *The Gift of Freedom*

As you practice letting go, you'll experience a profound shift in your perspective. You'll find yourself less burdened by anxiety and fear. Your heart will become a haven of peace, a sanctuary from the storms of life. You'll have more freedom to experience joy, connection, and fulfillment.

This isn't a passive process; it's an active choice you make every day. It's a commitment to living a life of authenticity, embracing the present moment, and finding freedom in the art of letting go.

# 6

## THE SPIRIT WITHIN

A wellspring of boundless love, wisdom, and peace lies within our being. This is the essence of our spirit, a divine spark connecting us to a universal source of light and energy. Beyond the fleeting labels and identities we adopt in this earthly realm, it is the core of who we are. This spirit is not something we acquire or achieve; it is our inherent nature, the foundation of our existence.

Imagine a vast ocean of pure love, wisdom, and peace—an unfathomable reservoir of tranquility and boundless potential. A tiny drop of this ocean resides within us, waiting to be recognized, nurtured, and allowed to flow freely. Our spirit is this drop, a shimmering jewel of pure consciousness, reflecting the infinite beauty and power of the divine source.

To connect with our spirit is to tap into this reservoir of inner peace. It is to experience the boundless love within us that radiates outward, touching all we encounter. It is to access the wisdom that guides us through life's complexities, providing clarity and insight into our choices. It is also important to find a profound sense of connection, a deep knowing that we are not alone but are part of something much more significant than ourselves.

The journey to connect with our spirit is inward, a quest for the true self that lies beneath the surface of our thoughts, emotions, and experiences. It is a journey of discovery, peeling back the layers of conditioning and conditioning to reveal the radiant being that resides within.

This journey requires a willingness to look within and to be honest with ourselves about our deepest desires and fears. It demands a commitment to shedding the masks we wear and embracing the authenticity that is our birthright. It calls for us to listen to the whispers of our intuition, the inner voice that guides us toward our true purpose and our most profound connection to the divine.

Through various spiritual practices, we can nurture our connection to our spirit. Meditation, prayer, contemplation, and acts of kindness are all pathways to access the depths of our being. These practices create a space within us where we can quiet the constant chatter of the mind and tap into the stillness and wisdom that reside within.

**Meditation**, in particular, can be a powerful tool for connecting with our spirit. Focusing on the present moment allows the mind to settle, creating a space for the spirit to emerge. As we sit in silence, we may experience peace and tranquility that transcends the limitations of our earthly experience.

**Prayer** is another way to connect with our spoken or unspoken spirit. It is a form of communication with a higher power, a way to express our gratitude, seek guidance, and surrender to a force greater than ourselves. Through prayer, we open ourselves to the love and support of the divine, reminding us that we are never truly alone.

**Contemplation**, reflecting on profound questions or spiritual truths, can also lead us deeper into our spirit. By pondering the mysteries of life and the nature of our being, we awaken a sense of wonder and awe that connects us to a universal source of wisdom and understanding.

**Acts of kindness**, performed with a spirit of love and compassion, are also a potent way to connect with the divine within us. When we extend ourselves to others, we tap into the wellspring of love that resides within, reminding us of our innate connection to all beings.

As we deepen our connection with our spirit, we experience the world differently. We see the beauty and wonder in every moment, recognizing the divine spark in all things. We feel a profound sense of peace and purpose, knowing that we are on the path to fulfilling our true potential.

This connection to our spirit is the foundation of a life lived in harmony, a life of peace and fulfillment. It is the source of our true strength, guiding light, and most profound connection to the universe.

To live from our spirit is to embrace the essence of who we indeed are. It is to shed the limitations of our ego and step into the boundless potential of our divine nature. It is to live a life of love, wisdom, and peace, knowing that we are an integral part of a vast, interconnected universe.

Cultivating a spiritual connection is like tending to a garden. It requires consistent effort, patience, and a willingness to nurture the inner seeds of peace within us. We can draw upon various spiritual practices to nourish our souls and strengthen our bond with the divine, the universal source of love, wisdom, and peace.

Meditation, a cornerstone of many spiritual traditions, provides a pathway to connect with our inner selves and tap into the serenity that lies within. We create space for clarity, insight, and a deep connection by quieting our minds and focusing on our breath. As we regularly practice meditation, we gradually cultivate a state of inner stillness where we can access a wellspring of wisdom and guidance.

Prayer, a form of communication with a higher power, can be an intimate and powerful way to cultivate spiritual connection. It allows us to express our gratitude, seek guidance, and release our burdens into the hands of a force greater than ourselves. Whether we pray silently or aloud, with words or simply with the intention of our heart, prayer can bring comfort, solace, and a sense of belonging.

Contemplation, a practice of deep reflection and introspection, allows us to delve into the depths of our being. We understand ourselves and our place in the universe by pondering on spiritual truths, contemplating our experiences, and examining our beliefs. Through contemplation, we can gain clarity on our life's purpose, connect with our inner wisdom, and find a sense of peace that transcends the chaos of the external world.

Spiritual practices are not confined to these traditional forms. We can also connect with our spirit through nature, immersing ourselves in the beauty and wonder of the natural world. A walk in a forest, the sound of the ocean waves, or the feeling of the sun on our skin can evoke a profound sense of connection and peace. Creative pursuits, such as painting, writing, music, or dance, can also serve as avenues for expressing our inner spirit and connecting with something beyond ourselves.

Ultimately, the path to a deeper spiritual connection is unique to each individual. There is no one right way to cultivate our inner spirit. The key lies in exploring various practices, finding what resonates with us, and committing to nurturing this connection through consistent effort and dedication. As we deepen our bond with our spirit, we unlock a wellspring of peace, love, and wisdom to guide us through life's challenges and illuminate our path toward a more fulfilling and meaningful existence. We discover that the trustworthy source of peace is not something we must achieve but rather something we must rediscover within ourselves.

Imagine a soft, gentle whisper, a subtle guiding force that speaks to you from within. This is the language of intuition, or for some, the Holy Spirit—a powerful and often underestimated source of inner wisdom. It's the voice of your soul, the echo of your highest self, offering insights and nudging you toward peace and fulfillment.

We often get caught up in the noise of the external world, bombarded by information, opinions, and demands. It's easy to lose touch with that inner voice, that quiet knowing that resides deep within. Yet, when we learn to listen and truly hear our intuition's whispers, we unlock a treasure trove of guidance, clarity, and peace.

Think of it like this: our intuition is like a compass, always pointing us towards our true north, our highest purpose. It's a natural guide that helps us navigate the complexities of life, making choices that align with our authentic selves.

But how do we learn to trust our intuition? It's a journey of self-discovery that requires us to quiet the mind's noise and cultivate a deeper connection with our inner self.

Here are some practices that can help:

**Practice Mindfulness:** Regular mindfulness meditation is a powerful tool for quieting the mind and becoming more attuned to the subtle whispers of intuition. We create space for our inner wisdom to emerge by focusing on the present moment.

**Cultivate Inner Stillness:** Take time each day for quiet reflection, allowing your mind to settle and your intuition to surface. This can be through journaling, prayer, nature walks, or silence.

**Pay Attention to Your Feelings:** Our intuition often communicates through our emotions. Notice the feelings that arise within you, particularly those that are subtle and persistent. Do you feel a sense of peace, joy, or excitement when considering a particular path? Or do you feel a sense of unease, fear, or anxiety? These feelings can offer valuable clues about what is aligned with your intuition.

**Trust Your Gut:** Often, our intuition whispers through that gut feeling, that sense of knowing that comes from deep within. Don't dismiss those gut feelings as mere hunches or coincidences. They are often the whispers of your soul, guiding you towards the right path.

**Seek Out Signs and Synchronicities:** Our intuition may communicate through synchronicities, seemingly coincidental events that appear to have a deeper meaning. Please pay attention to recurring themes, symbols, or messages in your life, as they may be subtle clues from your intuition.

**Practice Self-Reflection:** Regularly take time to reflect on your choices and decisions. Did your intuition guide you? How did you feel before, during, and after making those choices? This introspection helps you build trust in your inner wisdom.

**Trust the Process:** Learning to trust your intuition is a journey, not a destination. There will be times when you feel confident, and you doubt your inner voice. Be patient and continue cultivating a deeper connection with your intuition.

Remember, intuition is not a magic wand granting instant clarity and peace. It's a guide, a compass that points you toward your true north. As you learn to listen and trust your intuition, you'll discover a profound inner peace, clarity, and purpose.

You'll find yourself navigating life with a more profound sense of confidence, making choices that align with your authentic self, and living a life that aligns with your highest purpose. The language of intuition is beautiful and powerful. As you learn to speak and understand it, you unlock a world of possibilities and embark on a journey of profound self-discovery and inner peace.

The power of intention and visualization is a profound tool for aligning our thoughts and actions with our spiritual purpose. Imagine a seed in the fertile earth, dormant yet brimming with potential. Just as that seed holds within it the blueprint for a majestic tree, so too do we possess an inner blueprint, a vision of who we are meant to be and what we are meant to contribute to the world. Intention and visualization act as the sun and rain, nurturing this inner seed and guiding it to unfold into its full potential.

The intention is like planting a seed in our minds. It's a conscious choice to direct our energy towards a specific outcome. When we set an intention with clarity and conviction, we create a powerful vibration that attracts the necessary circumstances and resources to manifest our desires. Imagine, for instance, a painter intending to create a masterpiece. This intention is not just a fleeting thought; it's a commitment, a powerful force that drives their creative process. They begin to see their vision in their mind's eye, envisioning every brushstroke, every color, every detail. This visualization fuels their passion, guiding their hand as they bring their artistic vision to life.

Visualization is seeing our desired outcome in our mind's eye. It's a potent practice that allows us to experience the feeling of our dreams as if they were already a reality. We create a vivid mental image of the life we want to live, the goals we want to achieve, the relationships we want to nurture. This mental rehearsal engages our emotions, aligning our thoughts and actions with our desires. Visualizing ourselves as peaceful, joyful, and loving beings strengthens our inner resolve to embody these qualities daily.

The combination of intention and visualization creates a synergy that propels us toward our spiritual goals. It's as if we're sending a message to the universe, declaring our desire and aligning our energy with its manifestation. The more we visualize, the more we engage our subconscious mind, which operates on a level beyond conscious thought. The subconscious mind is like fertile soil, ready to receive the seeds of our intentions and nurture them into fruition. The more we cultivate a positive, hopeful mindset, the more likely we attract positive experiences and opportunities.

Consider the story of a young woman who dreamed of becoming a musician. From a young age, she imagined performing on grand stages, sharing her music with the world. She visualized herself holding a guitar, her fingers effortlessly gliding across the strings, composing melodies that touched hearts and moved souls. She practiced diligently, honing her skills, and her passion fuelled her determination. She attracted the resources she needed to develop her talent through her unwavering intention and consistent visualization. Eventually, she fulfilled her dream, bringing her music to life on large and small stages.

Intention and visualization are not mere exercises in wishful thinking; they are potent tools for aligning our consciousness with our spiritual purpose. By setting clear intentions and visualizing our desired outcomes, we tap into the infinite possibilities within us, aligning our actions with our deepest aspirations. It's like a compass, guiding us through the often turbulent waters of life, reminding us of our true north, the path to peace and fulfillment.

Here are some practical tips for incorporating intention and visualization into your daily life:

**You should set clear intentions:** Begin by identifying your most heartfelt desires. What are your goals, both personal and spiritual? What kind of life do you want to create? When setting intentions, be specific, using positive affirmations and phrases that resonate with your heart.

**Create a vision board:** A visual representation of your dreams and aspirations. Collect images, quotes, and affirmations that symbolize your goals and passions. Place this board in a prominent location where you can see it daily, constantly reminding you of your aspirations.

**Practice visualization regularly:** Find a quiet place to relax and focus. Close your eyes and imagine yourself living the life you desire. Visualize yourself experiencing joy, peace, and fulfillment. Engage all your senses, feeling the emotions associated with your dreams as if they were already a reality.

**Use affirmations:** Positive affirmations are powerful statements that reprogram our subconscious mind, replacing negative thoughts with empowering beliefs. Repeat affirmations daily, focusing on gratitude and abundance associated with your desires.

**Be patient and persistent:** Manifesting our intentions and visualizing our dreams takes time and consistent effort. Be patient with yourself, trust the process, and remain committed to your goals.

By aligning our thoughts and actions with our spiritual purpose through intention and visualization, we open ourselves to the possibility of living a life filled with meaning, joy, and peace. We become active participants in creating our reality, guided by the wisdom of our spirit and the boundless potential within us.

## Living from the Heart: A Spiritually Guided Life

Imagine a life where every decision, every action, and every thought is guided by an inner compass, a profound connection to your true essence—your spirit. This is the essence of living from the heart, a way of being that transcends the limitations of the mind and connects you to the boundless source of peace, love, and wisdom that resides within.

Living from the heart isn't about suppressing emotions or ignoring the complexities of life. Instead, it's about cultivating a deep awareness, allowing intuition, or the Holy Spirit to guide you, and aligning your actions with your core values and beliefs. This is a journey of self-discovery, a path of transformation where you become the architect of your peace and fulfillment.

<u>Here are some practical tips and insights for embracing a spiritually guided life</u>:

**Listen to Your Inner Voice, the Holy Spirit:**

Within you lies a wellspring of wisdom, a guiding force that whispers through your intuition. This inner voice is often subtle but always present, offering guidance and clarity on your path. Take time to quiet your mind, connect with your breath, and listen. Pay attention to the feelings, sensations, and thoughts that arise within you. These are the whispers of your soul, leading you toward your true purpose and a life of deeper meaning.

**Embrace Your Spiritual Practices:**

Spiritual practices, such as meditation, prayer, and contemplation, serve as pathways to connect with your inner source of peace. These practices provide a space for reflection, introspection, and a deeper understanding of your spiritual nature. Regularly engaging in these practices helps you cultivate a sense of inner calm, clarity, and connection to something larger than yourself.

**Align Your Actions with Your Values:**

Living from the heart requires aligning your actions with your core values and beliefs. Ask yourself: What are the principles that guide my life? What are my priorities? When your actions align with your values, you create a sense of inner unity, leading to greater peace and satisfaction.

**Embrace Gratitude and Appreciation:**

A heart filled with gratitude and appreciation naturally radiates peace. Make a conscious effort to acknowledge the good things in your life, big or small. Express gratitude for the people in your life, the blessings you receive, and the beauty surrounding you. This practice shifts your focus from lack to abundance, fostering a sense of contentment and inner peace.

**Practice Self-Compassion and Acceptance:**

Living from the heart means treating yourself with kindness, compassion, and understanding. Be gentle with yourself, acknowledge your strengths and weaknesses, and accept your imperfections.

Self-compassion allows you to release self-criticism and move forward with love and acceptance.

**Cultivate Kindness and Forgiveness:**

Extending kindness and forgiveness to others creates a ripple effect of peace. Treating others with empathy and understanding creates a more harmonious environment for yourself and those around you. Forgiveness is a powerful tool for releasing resentment and creating space for healing and reconciliation.

**Live in the Present Moment:**

Living from the heart requires being fully present in the moment. The past is gone, and the future is yet to come. By cultivating mindfulness, you can find peace in the present moment, appreciating the beauty and richness of life right now.

**Trust the Flow of Life:**

Living from the heart means surrendering to the flow of life, trusting in events unfolding, and releasing control. It's about recognizing that you're not always in control and embracing the unexpected turns that life may take. This surrender allows you to find peace in the unknown, knowing everything is happening exactly as it should.

**Embrace Your Purpose and Passion:**

Living a spiritually guided life means aligning your actions with your purpose and passions. Ask yourself: What ignites my soul?

What am I meant to do with my life? Pursuing your purpose and living with love creates a sense of fulfillment and deep inner peace.

**Connect with Nature:**

Spending time in nature has a profound calming effect on the mind and spirit. The natural world offers peace, awe, and wonder, reminding us of our interconnectedness to life. Walk barefoot on the earth, breathe in the fresh air, and feel the energy of the natural world nourishing your soul.

Living from the heart is a journey of continuous growth and self-discovery. It's a path of inner peace, fulfillment, and alignment with your true essence. By embracing the principles and practices outlined above, you can cultivate a life guided by your spirit, leading to a more profound sense of purpose, connection, and inner peace.

# 7

# THE INTERCONNECTEDNESS OF PEACE

The interconnectedness of peace is a profound truth at the heart of our existence. It is not merely a concept but a living reality that unfolds within us and extends outward into the world. When we speak of peace, we are not simply referring to the absence of conflict but to a deep and enduring state of harmony that encompasses every aspect of our being. This inner harmony is not a distant aspiration but a tangible state of being that we can cultivate through mindful intention and dedicated practice.

Imagine a serene lake, its surface reflecting the azure sky and the surrounding greenery. Its tranquility is not merely the absence of waves but a profound stillness that permeates the very essence of the water. Similarly, inner peace is not the absence of negative thoughts or challenging emotions but a profound serenity within our very being. It is the unshakeable foundation upon which we navigate the storms of life, finding solace and strength amidst adversity.

This inner peace, however, does not exist in isolation. It is intrinsically connected to our outer world, influencing our relationships, actions, and impact on the world around us. When we cultivate inner peace, we become vessels of tranquility, radiating a calming presence that can positively affect those around us. We become more understanding, more empathetic, and more capable of seeing the world through a lens of compassion and forgiveness.

The ripple effect of inner peace extends far beyond our personal lives. It is the seed from which a more peaceful world can blossom. Imagine a world where individuals have cultivated a sense of inner peace, their actions are guided by compassion and understanding, and conflicts are resolved through dialogue and collaboration. This is the potential that each of us holds within us, the power to create a more peaceful world one heart at a time.

This interconnectedness of peace is not simply a romantic ideal but a practical reality we can experience daily. When we choose to respond to conflict with patience and understanding, practice forgiveness instead of holding onto resentment, and extend kindness and compassion to those around us, we are actively contributing to a more peaceful world. Each act of kindness, each moment of forgiveness, and each act of selfless service becomes a small step toward a world where peace prevails.

The challenge, however, lies in recognizing that this journey to a peaceful world begins within us. We can genuinely contribute to a more harmonious world by cultivating inner peace. This is not about suppressing our emotions or ignoring our challenges but about learning to navigate them with grace, compassion, and a deep sense of inner stillness.

Imagine a garden where the seeds of peace are planted. The soil of our hearts is fertile ground, and the seeds of compassion, understanding, and forgiveness are ready to blossom. With each act of kindness and each moment of mindfulness, we nurture these seeds, allowing them to grow into vibrant flowers of peace that will ultimately transform our world.

The world is a complex tapestry woven with threads of interconnectedness. Each individual, each relationship, and each action contribute to the overall pattern. When we cultivate inner peace, we become part of a grand tapestry of peace woven with threads of compassion, forgiveness, and understanding. This is the legacy we leave behind, the gift of peace we share with the world.

To truly understand the interconnectedness of peace, we must embrace the idea that our actions, thoughts, and feelings ripple outward, influencing the world around us. We cannot separate ourselves from this interconnected web of life. We are all part of a larger ecosystem of peace, where our actions, however small, have the potential to create a ripple effect of positive change.

Let us, therefore, embrace the journey of inner peace, knowing that it is not just about finding solace for ourselves but about becoming a beacon of peace for the world. Let us nurture the seeds of peace within us, allowing them to blossom into a vibrant garden of love, compassion, and understanding. Let us be the change we wish to see in the world, one peaceful step at a time.

The ability to empathize with others, to truly understand their perspectives and experiences is a cornerstone of peaceful relationships. Empathy involves stepping outside of our self-centered lens and stepping into the shoes of another. It requires us to suspend judgment, to listen with an open heart, and to see the world through their eyes.

This ability to understand is essential in a world often characterized by division and conflict. When we lack empathy, we view others as different, even adversaries. We build walls of prejudice, suspicion, and fear, making connecting and finding common ground difficult.

Empathy, however, bridges these divides. When we cultivate empathy, we recognize the shared humanity that binds us all. We see that others, despite their differences, are experiencing similar emotions, fears, hopes, and dreams.

This realization fosters compassion, a deep feeling of concern for the well-being of others. Compassion prompts us to act with kindness and understanding, to offer support and comfort to those in need.

Let's imagine a world where every interaction is infused with empathy. Imagine a world where we respond with understanding and compassion instead of reacting with anger or defensiveness.

Imagine a world where disagreements are met with open dialogue and a genuine desire to find solutions that work for everyone.

This is the world that empathy can create.

But empathy isn't simply a feeling; it's a practice. It requires conscious effort, especially when confronted with viewpoints or experiences that challenge our own. It requires us to listen actively, ask open-ended questions, and try to truly understand the other person's perspective.

This doesn't mean we must agree with everything someone says or does. It means that we can approach disagreements with respect and a genuine desire to bridge the gap.

Developing empathy can be a journey, but it's worth taking. By cultivating empathy, we deepen our connections with others and create a more peaceful and harmonious world.

Let's consider a few practical ways to cultivate empathy in our daily lives:

**Active Listening:** When someone shares their thoughts or feelings, practice active listening. Please put down your phone, make eye contact, and focus on what they say. Ask questions to clarify their perspective and demonstrate that you are genuinely interested in understanding their experience.

**Reading:** Expand your understanding of the world by reading books, articles, and stories that offer different perspectives. Explore cultures and lifestyles different from your own. By stepping outside your bubble, you can develop greater empathy and appreciation for the diversity of human experience.

**Meditation:** Meditation can cultivate a sense of interconnectedness and compassion. Practice mindfulness exercises to develop greater self-awareness and become more attuned to the emotions of those around you.

**Volunteer Work:** Volunteer in your community and engage with people from different backgrounds. Engage in service that allows you to connect with others and understand their challenges.

As we develop empathy, we plant peace in our relationships, communities, and the world. Empathy is not simply a personal virtue but a force for positive change.

Think of the positive impact of empathy in various situations:

**Parent-Child Relationships:** When parents practice empathy towards their children, they are more likely to understand their children's needs and motivations. This fosters stronger bonds and facilitates healthy communication, leading to peaceful and harmonious family dynamics.

**Workplace Environments:** Empathy is crucial for creating positive and productive work environments. When colleagues empathize with each other's challenges and perspectives, they are more likely to collaborate effectively and resolve conflicts constructively.

**Community Relations:** Empathy is essential for building bridges between different communities. By understanding the concerns, experiences, and values of others, we can foster a sense of shared purpose and create a more inclusive and peaceful society.

Empathy is a powerful tool for building a world based on understanding, compassion, and peace. It is vital for creating a world where differences are celebrated, conflicts are resolved peacefully, and everyone feels a sense of belonging and security.

The journey to a peaceful world starts within each of us. As we cultivate empathy and understanding, we contribute to a more peaceful and harmonious world.

Forgiveness is a powerful act of liberation, not only for the recipient but also for the forgiver. It is a conscious decision to release resentment, anger, and bitterness instead of letting go of the past and moving forward with a lighter heart. Forgiveness is not condoning the wrongdoings of others but rather choosing to break free from the chains of anger and bitterness that bind us. It is a choice to relinquish the burden of holding onto pain and to allow ourselves the space to heal and grow.

Forgiveness is crucial in building bridges of peace and understanding in interpersonal relationships. When we hold onto grudges, we create a chasm between ourselves and others, fostering a sense of separation and resentment. On the other hand, forgiveness acts as a bridge, allowing us to reconnect with those we may have hurt or been hurt by. It is a powerful tool for healing past wounds and creating a foundation for stronger, healthier relationships.

Beyond personal relationships, forgiveness is a vital force for global peace. When nations conflict, the seeds of anger, hatred, and mistrust take root, making reconciliation seem impossible. Forgiveness, in this context, transcends personal grievances and becomes a catalyst for collective healing. It is a commitment to letting go of the past, embracing understanding and compassion, and paving the way for a more peaceful future.

There are countless examples throughout history where acts of forgiveness have led to profound transformation and healing. The South African Truth and Reconciliation Commission, established after the end of apartheid, provided a platform for victims of state-sponsored violence to share their stories and for perpetrators to seek forgiveness. This act of collective forgiveness played a crucial role in healing the wounds of the past and building a foundation for a more just and equitable society.

The power of forgiveness lies in its ability to break the cycle of violence and hatred. When we choose to forgive, we interrupt the flow of negativity and create a space for peace to emerge. Forgiveness is not a weakness but rather an act of strength, a testament to our capacity for compassion and understanding.

Forgiveness is not always easy, and it may take time to release anger and resentment fully. However, the journey of forgiveness is transformative, leading to a more profound sense of peace, joy, and liberation. As we learn to forgive ourselves and others, we create a ripple effect of peace that extends far beyond our personal lives, touching the hearts of those around us and contributing to a more peaceful world.

## *The Process of Forgiveness*

Forgiving another person is a process that takes time, effort, and a willingness to let go. It is not about minimizing the pain or harm inflicted but rather about releasing its hold on you. Here are some steps that may be helpful in the journey of forgiveness:

**Acknowledge and Accept:** The first step is to acknowledge the hurt and pain you experienced. Allow yourself to feel the emotions fully, without judgment or suppression. Accept that you have been hurt and that it is okay to feel pain.

**Understand the Other Person's Perspective:** Try to understand the other person's perspective, even if you disagree with their actions. This doesn't mean excusing their behavior but instead recognizing that they may have had their reasons for acting as they did.

**Choose to Forgive:** Forgiveness is a choice. It is a decision to release the anger, resentment, and bitterness you hold onto. It is not about forgetting the past but choosing not to let it control you.

**Release the Pain:** Once you have forgiven, allow yourself to release the pain. Visualize the pain leaving your body, like a cloud dissipating in the sky. You may find it helpful to write a letter of forgiveness to the person you are trying to forgive, even if you don't plan to send it.

**Embrace Compassion and Understanding:** Forgiveness is about letting go of negative emotions and embracing compassion and understanding. Try cultivating empathy for others, even if you cannot fully understand their actions.

**Move Forward:** Forgiveness is a journey, not a destination. It is an ongoing process of letting go and moving forward. Allow yourself time to heal and to rebuild your life.

*Forgiving Yourself*

Just as we can forgive others, it is equally important to forgive ourselves. We all make mistakes, and it is essential to learn from them and move on. Holding onto guilt, shame, or regret can lead to self-destructive patterns and hinder our growth. Self-forgiveness is an act of self-love and acceptance. It is a recognition that we are all human and capable of growth and change.

Here are some steps for forgiving yourself:

**Acknowledge Your Mistakes:** The first step in forgiving yourself is acknowledging your mistakes. Don't deny or minimize them. Be honest with yourself about what you did and how it affected others.

**Learn from Your Mistakes:** Once you have acknowledged your mistakes, reflect on what you can learn from them. How can you avoid making the same mistakes in the future?

**Release the Guilt and Shame:** Guilt and shame can be crippling emotions. They can keep us stuck in the past and prevent us from moving forward. Choose to release these emotions and allow yourself to be free.

**Practice Self-Compassion:** Be kind to yourself. Remember that everyone makes mistakes. Treat yourself with the same compassion and understanding you would offer a loved one.

**Focus on the Present:** Instead of dwelling on the past, focus on the present moment. What can you do today to create a more positive and fulfilling life?

### *The Power of Reconciliation*

Forgiveness is often the first step towards reconciliation. Reconciliation involves repairing broken relationships and restoring harmony. It is a process of rebuilding trust, understanding, and communication. It is a commitment to moving forward together, acknowledging the past while focusing on creating a better future.

Tips for Reconciliation:

**Open and Honest Communication:** Reconciliation requires open and honest communication. Both parties must be willing to listen to each other's perspectives and express their feelings and needs.

**Taking Responsibility:** Both parties must take responsibility for their role in the conflict. This doesn't mean blaming or shaming but acknowledging your role.

**Apologizing Sincerely:** A sincere apology is often the first step towards reconciliation. It shows the other person that you are genuinely sorry for your actions and willing to make amends.

**Making Amends:** If possible, could you make amends for the harm you caused? This may involve taking concrete steps to repair the damage or to show the other person that you have changed.

**Forgiveness and Compassion:** Remember that reconciliation requires forgiveness and compassion. It would be best if you were willing to let go of the anger, resentment, and bitterness you may be holding onto.

## *The Ripple Effect of Peace*

When we cultivate inner peace and practice forgiveness, we create a ripple effect that extends far beyond ourselves. Our peaceful demeanor influences the people around us, creating a more harmonious and supportive environment. As we build bridges of understanding and compassion, we contribute to a more peaceful world.

The journey to peace is continuous, requiring ongoing self-reflection, practice, and commitment. It is a path that we embark upon for ourselves and the betterment of the world we share. Through our individual efforts to cultivate peace within, we can contribute to a collective shift in consciousness, creating a more just, compassionate, and harmonious world.

The pursuit of peace is a journey that extends beyond our personal lives. Just as a single ripple can create waves across a pond, our actions can contribute to a more significant movement for peace. Activism and advocacy, in all their forms, are essential in fostering a culture of peace and harmony.

Imagine a world where every person, regardless of background, ideology, or belief, embraces the principles of peace in their daily lives. Imagine communities united by empathy, compassion, and a shared desire for understanding. Such a world is not a romantic fantasy but a possibility we can collectively cultivate through dedicated efforts.

Activism for peace takes many forms. It can be as grand as organizing marches, lobbying for legislation, or supporting organizations working toward conflict resolution and social justice. It can also be as simple as engaging in peaceful dialogue, challenging prejudice and discrimination in our daily interactions, or advocating for non-violent solutions to conflict.

Volunteering is another powerful way to contribute to a peaceful world. Whether working with refugees, supporting peace education initiatives, or advocating for human rights, volunteering offers a tangible way to make a difference. By dedicating our time and energy to causes we believe in, we directly impact the lives of others and contribute to a more just and compassionate society.

But even without formal activism or volunteering, we can all live lives embodying the principles of peace. Treating others with kindness, understanding, and respect, regardless of their differences, can create positive energy. By practicing forgiveness, cultivating empathy, and seeking common ground, we can build a more peaceful and harmonious world, one interaction at a time.

The pursuit of peace is not a spectator sport. We are all called to participate in this journey, whether through active engagement, quiet contemplation, or simply choosing to live a life that embodies the principles of peace. It is a journey that starts within but extends outwards, connecting us to a broader tapestry of humanity.

Every act of kindness, every word of understanding, every moment of peace we cultivate within ourselves and share with others contributes to the tapestry of a more peaceful world. Let us be the weavers of this tapestry, stitching together a future where peace is not a distant dream but a shared reality.

Imagine a world where the air hums with kindness, disputes are resolved with understanding, and cooperation and compassion are the norm. This vision of a peaceful world isn't a romantic fantasy but a possibility we can actively cultivate, starting with our hearts and minds.

The journey to a peaceful world begins with understanding the interconnectedness of inner and outer peace. The ripple effect of inner peace radiates outward, impacting our relationships, communities, and the world.

In our personal lives, cultivating a culture of peace starts with a conscious effort to embody peace in our interactions.

**Embrace Active Listening:** Practice genuinely listening to understand another's perspective, setting aside our preconceptions and judgments. This requires patience, empathy, and a willingness to see the world through another's eyes.

**Embrace Nonviolent Communication:** Opt for language that focuses on needs and feelings, avoiding accusatory or judgmental tones. This creates an atmosphere of mutual respect and encourages open dialogue.

**Practice Forgiveness and Reconciliation:** Forgiveness doesn't mean condoning wrongdoings but releasing resentment and bitterness that hold us hostage. It opens the door to healing and allows for the possibility of reconciliation.

**Cultivate Gratitude and Appreciation:** Expressing gratitude and appreciation for the good in our lives shifts our focus from what's lacking to what we have. This fosters a sense of contentment and peace within ourselves and inspires generosity towards others.

**Resolve Conflicts Constructively:** When disagreements arise, you can approach them with a desire for understanding and a willingness to compromise. Seek common ground, listen to each other's perspectives, and explore creative solutions that benefit everyone.

**Extend Kindness and Compassion:** Simple acts of kindness, such as offering a helping hand, a listening ear, or a genuine smile, can have a profound impact on others. It fosters a sense of connection and strengthens our collective understanding of community. Beyond our relationships, we can actively contribute to a culture of peace in our wider communities and workplaces.

**Promote Peace Education:** Support initiatives that promote peace education in schools, workplaces, and communities. These programs can equip individuals with the knowledge, skills, and values necessary to navigate conflicts peacefully and build bridges of understanding.

**Advocate for Nonviolent Conflict Resolution:** Support organizations and initiatives promoting nonviolent conflict resolution, mediating disputes, and finding peaceful solutions.

**Support Peacebuilding Initiatives:** Contribute to organizations addressing the root causes of conflict, such as poverty, inequality, and social injustice. These efforts are crucial for creating lasting peace and building a more equitable world.

**Create Spaces for Dialogue and Understanding:** Encourage dialogue and understanding across cultural and ideological differences. Create platforms where people can share their perspectives, listen to one another, and build bridges of empathy and connection.

**Promote Environmental Sustainability:** A peaceful world is one where we live harmoniously with nature. Support efforts to protect the environment, reduce carbon footprint, and promote sustainable practices.

Our actions may seem small, but collectively, they can create a ripple effect of peace extending far beyond our personal lives. Living with compassion, understanding, and a commitment to peace creates a world where everyone can thrive.

As Mahatma Gandhi said, "Be the change you want to see in the world." We become beacons of hope and inspiration for others by cultivating peace within ourselves. Each step we take, no matter how small, contributes to creating a more peaceful world for all.

# 8

## MEDITATION AND MINDFULNESS

Meditation and mindfulness are powerful tools for calming the mind, reducing stress, and fostering inner peace. They invite us to step back from the constant chatter of thoughts and connect with a more profound sense of presence and stillness. Meditation is not about emptying the mind but observing the flow of thoughts without judgment, allowing them to pass like clouds in the sky. It's about creating a space of awareness and tranquility within ourselves.

There are many different forms of meditation, from guided meditations with specific themes to silent meditations focused on breath or a mantra. The key is to find a practice that resonates with you and helps you cultivate a state of calm and focus.

*Finding Your Meditation Style:*

**Guided Meditation** involves following a voice that leads you through visualizations, affirmations, or breathwork exercises. Guided meditations can be beneficial for beginners as they provide structure and guidance. You can find a wealth of guided meditations online or through apps.

**Mindfulness Meditation:** This practice involves paying attention to the present moment without judgment. You might focus on your breath, bodily sensations, or the sounds around you, simply observing without getting carried away by thoughts.

**Mantra Meditation** involves repeating a word, phrase, or sound silently or aloud. The repetition helps to focus the mind and calm the nervous system.

**Walking Meditation:** This combines physical movement with mindfulness. As you walk slowly and intentionally, you pay attention to the sensations of your feet on the ground, your breath, and your surroundings.

*Setting the Stage for Meditation:*

**Find a Quiet Space:** Choose a peaceful and comfortable place where you won't be disturbed. It could be your bedroom, a meditation room, or a quiet natural corner.

**Create a Comfortable Setting:** Make sure you're comfortable. You can sit on a cushion or chair or lie down. Wear loose-fitting clothes and make sure the temperature is comfortable.

**Set a Timer:** Start with short meditation sessions, perhaps 5 to 10 minutes, and gradually increase the time as you become more comfortable.

**Minimize Distractions:** Turn off your phone, computer, and other distractions.

### *The Art of Focused Breathing:*

**Belly Breathing:** This technique helps to calm the nervous system and reduce anxiety. Sit or lie comfortably; place one hand on your belly and the other on your chest. Inhale deeply through your nose, expanding your belly like a balloon. Exhale slowly through your mouth, letting your belly deflate.

**Box Breathing:** This rhythmic breathing pattern promotes relaxation and focus. Inhale slowly for a count of 4, hold your breath for a count of 4, exhale slowly for a count of 4, and hold your breath again for a count of 4. Repeat this cycle for several minutes.

**Alternate Nostril Breathing:** This technique helps balance the body's energy. Close your right nostril with your thumb and inhale slowly through your left nostril. Close your left nostril with your ring finger and exhale through your right nostril. Inhale through your right nostril, close it with your thumb, and exhale through your left nostril. Repeat this cycle for several minutes.

### *Embracing Mindfulness:*

**Body Scan:** Pay attention to different body parts, starting from your toes and moving upwards. Please look at any sensations, such as warmth, tingling, or tension, without judgment.

**Mindful Walking:** Bring your attention to the sensations of your feet on the ground, your breath, and your surroundings as you walk slowly and intentionally.

**Mindful Eating:** Pay attention to your food's taste, smell, and texture as you eat. Please look at the process of chewing and swallowing without rushing or distractions.

*Overcoming Distractions:*

**Don't Judge Yourself:** It's normal for your mind to wander during meditation. When you notice your thoughts drifting, gently bring your attention to your breath or chosen focus.

**Be Patient:** Developing a regular meditation routine takes time and practice. Keep going even if you find it challenging at first.

**Seek Guidance:** If you're struggling with meditation, consider seeking guidance from a qualified teacher or joining a meditation group.

*Integrating Mindfulness into Daily Life:*

**Mindful Moments:** Throughout the day, take a few moments to pause and bring your attention to the present moment. Notice your breath, your body, and your surroundings.

**Mindful Activities:** Practice mindfulness while engaging in everyday activities like washing dishes, driving, or walking.

**Mindful Communication:** Listen to your thoughts and emotions during conversations, and listen to others with empathy and understanding.

Meditation and mindfulness are not quick fixes but a lifelong journey of self-discovery and inner peace. With practice and patience, you can develop a deeper connection with yourself, cultivate a calm and focused mind, and find a lasting sense of peace within.

Deep breathing is a powerful tool for calming the mind, regulating emotions, and promoting relaxation. It works by influencing the nervous system and slowing down the heart rate, which can help reduce anxiety and stress. Many different deep breathing techniques can be incorporated into your daily routine to cultivate inner peace.

Here are a few examples:

**Diaphragmatic Breathing**

This technique, also known as belly breathing, is one of the most basic and practical deep breathing exercises. It focuses on using the diaphragm, the large muscle below the lungs, to facilitate deep, rhythmic breaths.

1. **Find a comfortable position:** Sit or lie down in a relaxed posture.

2. **Place one hand on your chest and the other on your belly.** Your belly should rise as you inhale while your chest

remains relatively still.

3. **Inhale slowly and deeply through your nose:** Count to four as you breathe in, allowing your belly to expand.

4. **Exhale slowly through your mouth:** Count to four as you breathe, allowing your belly to contract gently.

5. **Repeat:** Continue this rhythmic breathing for several minutes, focusing on the sensations of your breath.

## Box Breathing

Box breathing is a simple yet powerful technique that helps to regulate the breath and promote calmness. It is often used by military personnel to manage stress and maintain focus.

1. **Inhale slowly and deeply through your nose.** Count to four as you breathe in.

2. **Hold your breath:** Count to four while holding your breath.

3. **Exhale slowly through your mouth.** Count to four as you breathe out.

4. **Hold your breath:** Count to four while holding your breath.

5. **Repeat:** Continue this breathing pattern for several minutes, focusing on the rhythm of your breath.

## Alternate Nostril Breathing

Alternate nostril breathing, also known as Nadi Shodhana, is used in yoga and meditation to balance energy and promote calmness. It involves breathing through one nostril at a time, alternating between the two sides.

1. **Sit comfortably:** Find a comfortable seated position with your spine straight.

2. **Close your right nostril with your right thumb:** Inhale deeply through your left nostril.

3. **Close your left nostril with your ring and little fingers.** Exhale through your right nostril.

4. **Inhale through your right nostril:** Count to four as you breathe in.

5. **Close your right nostril:** Exhale through your left nostril, counting to four.

6. **Repeat:** Continue alternating between the nostrils for several minutes, focusing on the sensations of your breath.

## Lion's Breath

This powerful breathing technique stimulates the nervous system, releasing tension and promoting mental clarity. It involves exhaling forcefully through the mouth, mimicking the roar of a lion.

1. **Sit comfortably:** Find a comfortable seated position with your spine straight.

2. **Inhale deeply through your nose.** Count to four as you breathe in.

3. **Exhale forcefully through your mouth:** Open your mouth wide, stick out your tongue, and exhale with a strong "ha" sound as if roaring like a lion.

4. **Repeat:** Continue this breathing pattern for several minutes, focusing on releasing tension with each exhalation.

## 4-7-8 Breathing

This simple yet effective breathing technique promotes relaxation and reduces anxiety. It involves a specific breathing pattern that helps slow the heart rate and calm the nervous system.

1. **Close your eyes and relax:** Find a comfortable seated position with your spine straight.

2. **Exhale completely through your mouth:** Let out all the air in your lungs.

3. **Inhale quietly through your nose:** Count to four as

you breathe in.

4. **Hold your breath:** Count to seven while holding your breath.

5. **Exhale entirely through your mouth:** Count to eight as you breathe out.

6. **Repeat:** Continue this breathing pattern for several minutes, focusing on the rhythm of your breath.

## *The Power of Breath*

Deep breathing techniques offer a powerful way to influence our physiological and mental states. By consciously regulating our breath, we can activate the parasympathetic nervous system, which promotes relaxation, calmness, and a sense of well-being. Regularly practicing these techniques can help reduce stress, anxiety, and tension, allowing us to better understand inner peace and harmony.

It's important to note that while deep breathing can be a valuable tool for managing stress and anxiety, it's not a substitute for professional medical advice or treatment. If you are experiencing severe anxiety or other mental health challenges, it's essential to seek guidance from a qualified healthcare professional.

## *Integrating Breathwork into Daily Life*

Deep breathing techniques can be incorporated into your daily routine in various ways. You can practice the following:

**In the morning:** Start your day with a few minutes of deep breathing to set a calm and focused intention.

**Before bed:** Practice deep breathing to relax your mind and body before sleep.

**During stressful situations:** When feeling overwhelmed, take a few deep breaths to calm your nerves and regain composure.

**Throughout the day:** Use deep breathing as a mini meditation to alleviate stress and cultivate inner peace.

Tips for Effective Breathing

**Find a quiet place:** Choose a peaceful environment where you can focus on your breath without distractions.

**Focus on your breath:** Pay attention to the sensations of your breath as they enter and exit your body.

**Be patient:** It takes time and practice to master deep breathing techniques. Keep going even if you don't see results immediately.

**Listen to your body:** If you experience discomfort, stop the exercise and adjust your breathing pattern.

**Enjoy the process:** Approach deep breathing with curiosity and openness, allowing the practice to become a source of peace and tranquility.

Deep breathing is a simple yet powerful tool that can be used to cultivate inner harmony. By consciously regulating our breath, we can unlock many benefits, including reduced stress, improved focus, and a greater sense of peace and well-being. Regularly practicing these techniques can transform our relationship with ourselves, allowing us to navigate life's challenges with greater resilience and serenity.

The ancient wisdom of yoga, spanning millennia, offers a profound path to inner peace by harmonizing the body, mind, and spirit. Yoga, meaning "union" in Sanskrit, transcends physical exercise; it's a holistic practice that awakens the body's intelligence and cultivates a deep sense of well-being. Through mindful movement, breath control, and meditation, yoga unlocks a reservoir of inner peace that radiates outward into all aspects of our lives.

Imagine standing on a yoga mat, the soft fabric grounding you to the earth. As you inhale, a gentle expansion fills your lungs, a sense of spaciousness permeating your being. With each exhale, you release tension, worries, and anxieties, leaving behind a calmness that settles within. The poses you practice, flowing seamlessly from one to another, invite you to explore the limits of your physical body while cultivating a sense of awareness and presence.

Yoga is more than just physical postures; it's a journey of self-discovery and self-acceptance. As you navigate different postures, you learn to listen to your body's whispers, honoring its boundaries and respecting its limitations. This process fosters a deep body awareness, a key ingredient in inner peace. Yoga encourages you to let go of the striving and pushing, inviting you to embrace the present moment with acceptance and gratitude.

Beyond the physical realm, yoga delves into the realm of the mind. Through focused breathing techniques like Pranayama, you learn to control your breath, a powerful tool for calming the mind and quieting the constant chatter of thoughts. This conscious breathwork helps cultivate a sense of stillness and focus, allowing you to observe your thoughts without judgment. As you practice, you begin to recognize the patterns of your mind, the thoughts that lead to stress, anxiety, or fear.

Yoga's profound impact extends to the realm of emotions. By cultivating a mindful awareness of your body, you gain a deeper understanding of the subtle nuances of your emotional landscape. You learn to observe the rise and fall of emotions without identifying with them, recognizing that emotions are transient, like waves that ebb and flow. This detachment from emotions, cultivated through yoga, allows you to experience more excellent emotional stability and peace.

Yoga also emphasizes the importance of connection between ourselves and others. Through various postures and practices, yoga encourages you to move beyond the isolation of the mind and connect with your own body, honoring the wisdom it holds. This connection to your body lays the foundation for deeper connections with others, cultivating empathy, compassion, and understanding.

Beyond yoga, countless other forms of movement can contribute to inner peace. With its expressive freedom and joyful energy, dance can be a powerful tool for releasing pent-up emotions and connecting with your inner spirit. Martial arts, focusing on discipline and self-control, can cultivate a sense of inner strength and calm. Even a simple walk in nature, allowing your body to move in sync with the rhythm of the Earth, can awaken a sense of peace and tranquility.

The key to finding peace through movement lies in the intention behind your actions. You unlock a transformative power when you approach movement with conscious awareness, seeking physical fitness and inner harmony. Movement becomes a form of meditation, a journey of self-discovery and self-acceptance.

Whether you choose yoga, dance, martial arts, or simply a stroll, the benefits of movement are undeniable. By integrating movement into your life, you cultivate a sense of well-being that radiates outward, influencing your thoughts, emotions, and interactions with the world.

The path to inner peace is sometimes linear but worth the journey. Through movement, we can awaken the body's inherent wisdom, harness the power of the mind, and cultivate a deep sense of peace that permeates every aspect of our being. As you move, be present. Be mindful. Be at peace.

Imagine a hidden room within your mind, a vault filled with the blueprints of your life. These blueprints, etched in the deepest recesses of your subconscious, dictate your thoughts, emotions, and actions. They shape your perception of the world and determine your reactions to life's ups and downs. Now, imagine the power of unlocking this vault, of reprogramming these blueprints with positive affirmations and vibrant visualizations. These practices' transformative potential is a potent alchemy that can unlock a reservoir of inner peace and well-being.

Positive affirmations are like seeds of positive change, planted directly into the fertile soil of your subconscious mind. They are concise statements of belief, uttered with conviction and repeated regularly that gradually rewire your mental circuitry. Each repetition reinforces the desired outcome, gently nudging your subconscious mind to align with your proclaiming empowering truths.

For instance, if you struggle with anxiety, instead of allowing those fearful thoughts to run rampant, you can cultivate peace by repeating affirmations like: "I am calm and peaceful," "I am strong and resilient," or "I release all fear and anxiety." With consistent practice, these affirmations take root in your subconscious, transforming your internal dialogue from fear to strength and serenity.

On the other hand, visualizations are like vivid paintings that your mind creates, vivid images of the life you aspire to live. They tap into the boundless creativity of your imagination, allowing you to experience peace and well-being before it manifests in reality. By visualizing yourself in peaceful and joyful scenarios, you stimulate your subconscious mind to align with these positive images, paving the way for them to become your reality.

Imagine, for example, that you are struggling with a problematic relationship. Instead of dwelling on the conflict, you can visualize a harmonious and loving interaction with the individual. Picture a calm and peaceful conversation where understanding and empathy bridge the gap between you. As you visualize this scene repeatedly, your subconscious mind begins to accept this harmonious outcome as a possibility, opening the door to more peaceful and fulfilling interactions in reality.

The power of positive affirmations and visualizations lies in their ability to bypass the conscious mind's resistance and work directly with the subconscious. When repeated regularly, they gradually shift your core beliefs and create a new internal framework for peace and well-being.

However, it's crucial to approach these practices with intention and sincerity. Empty words uttered without conviction will hold little power. To unlock their true transformative potential, infuse your affirmations and visualizations with genuine belief and heartfelt desire. Picture yourself in the state of peace and well-being you seek, feel the emotions associated with that state, and fully immerse yourself in the experience.

Also, please be patient and persistent. The journey to reprogramming your subconscious mind is not a sprint but a marathon. It requires consistent practice and unwavering commitment. Embrace the journey, allowing yourself to witness the subtle shifts in your thoughts, emotions, and actions as you cultivate a more profound sense of peace.

<u>Here are some additional strategies to enhance the effectiveness of positive affirmations and visualizations:</u>

**Specificity:** When crafting affirmations, be specific about the desired outcome. Instead of saying, "I am happy," try, "I feel joy and contentment in every moment."

**Positive Language:** Use positive language that focuses on what you want rather than what you don't want. For example, instead of saying, "I am not afraid," say, "I am confident and secure."

**Present Tense:** Formulate affirmations in the present tense as if they are already happening. This reinforces the belief that the desired outcome is already within your grasp.

**Emotional Connection:** Connect emotionally to your affirmations and visualizations. Feel the emotions you want to experience as if they are happening now.

**Visualize in Detail:** Create a vivid and detailed picture in your mind. Engage all your senses, including sight, sound, touch, taste, and smell, to make the experience more immersive.

**Practice Regularly:** The key to seeing results is consistency. Make time each day to practice your affirmations and visualizations, even just a few minutes.

**Be Patient:** Change takes time. Keep going if you see immediate results. Trust the process and keep practicing.

The path to inner peace is paved with self-discovery and self-transformation. Positive affirmations and visualizations offer powerful tools for navigating this journey, allowing you to rewrite the blueprints of your subconscious mind and create a life filled with inner harmony and well-being. Embrace these practices with intention, persistence, and an unwavering belief in your ability to make the peace you seek. The journey to peace begins within.

Creating a peaceful environment is not merely about surrounding yourself with calming décor or minimizing noise. It's a conscious effort to cultivate a space that supports your inner peace and allows you to thrive. This applies to your home, workplace, and personal interactions with others. Think of it as building a sanctuary for your mind, body, and spirit.

### *Your Home: A Sanctuary for Peace*

Imagine returning home after a long day, not just to a physical space, but to a haven of tranquility. Your home can become a refuge where you can unwind, recharge, and reconnect with yourself. Here's how you can create that atmosphere:

**Mindful Decluttering:** Clutter creates mental chaos. Please take the time to declutter your space, eliminating anything that doesn't serve you. This could include items that bring back negative memories, things you no longer need, or excessive stuff that overwhelms your senses. As you declutter, visualize releasing negativity and creating a clean slate for peace.

**Creating a Calming Color Palette:** Colors profoundly affect our emotions. Opt for soft, soothing hues like pastel blues, greens, and lavender. These colors promote relaxation and calm. Avoid overly bright or stimulating colors in your primary living areas.

**Bringing in Nature:** The presence of nature is a potent antidote to stress. Add houseplants to your home; their greenery and natural forms can give you a sense of tranquility. Incorporate natural materials like wood and stone in your décor, and if possible, create a small outdoor space where you can enjoy the fresh air and sounds of nature.

**Creating a Soothing Atmosphere:** Consider comfortable seating, soft lighting, and calming scents. Essential oils like lavender, chamomile, and sandalwood can create a peaceful ambiance. Consider soft, calming music or nature sounds to enhance relaxation.

**Creating a Meditation Space:** Dedicate a specific area in your home to meditation, even if it's just a tiny corner. This space should be free of distractions and inviting to you. You can add a cushion, a comfortable chair, or a small altar.

**Mindful Décor:** Surround yourself with objects that inspire peace and joy. This could be artwork, photos of loved ones, meaningful quotes, or anything that brings you a sense of serenity.

*Cultivating Peace at Work*

The workplace can be a breeding ground for stress and conflict. However, you can create an atmosphere of peace and harmony even in a demanding environment.

**Mindful Breathing:** Take a few deep breaths throughout the day, especially when feeling overwhelmed. Focusing on your breath brings you back to the present moment and helps to calm your nervous system.

**Creating a Personal Space:** Even in a shared office environment, make a small space that feels personal. Add a plant, a photo, or a small piece of artwork that brings you joy.

**Positive Communication:** Practice conscious communication with your colleagues. Listen attentively, speak with respect, and avoid negativity. Focus on finding solutions rather than highlighting problems.

**Mindful Breaks:** Take regular daily breaks to recharge from your work. This could be a short walk, a few moments of meditation, or simply a break to enjoy a cup of tea.

**Setting Boundaries:** Learn to say no to requests that overwhelm you or cannot realistically fulfill them. Protecting your time and energy helps to maintain a sense of balance and peace.

**Gratitude Practices:** Take a moment each day to reflect on what you are grateful for at work. This could be a successful project, a supportive colleague, or even a simple moment of peace.

### *Peaceful Relationships: The Building Blocks of Inner Harmony*

The people we choose to surround ourselves with have a profound impact on our emotional well-being. Cultivating peaceful relationships is essential for maintaining inner peace.

**Conscious Communication:** Listen empathetically, express yourself clearly, and strive for understanding. Avoid blaming, judging, or criticizing. Engage in open and honest conversations.

**Forgiveness and Letting Go:** Holding onto anger, resentment, or bitterness only harms yourself. Practice forgiveness, not just for others, but for yourself as well. Let go of the past and move forward with grace and understanding.

**Compassion and Empathy:** Put yourself in the other person's shoes, trying to understand their perspective and experiences. Treat others with kindness and respect, even when you disagree.

**Setting Boundaries:** Clearly define what you are comfortable with in a relationship. This helps to create a healthy balance and prevent resentment.

**Positive Affirmations:** Use positive affirmations to cultivate healthy and loving relationships. Affirmations like "Loving and supportive people surround me" or "I am open to receiving love and kindness" can help to create a more peaceful dynamic in your relationships.

**Giving and Receiving Love:** Nurturing your relationships through acts of kindness, generosity, and love is a powerful way to cultivate peace.

### *A World of Peace, Starting Within*

Creating a peaceful environment is a continuous process that requires intention, mindfulness, and a commitment to inner harmony. It's about creating a physical and emotional space where peace can flourish. By cultivating peace in your home, workplace, and relationships, you are enhancing your well-being and contributing to a more peaceful world. Remember, peace is a choice; cultivating it in your life makes you a beacon of peace for others.

# 9

## THE INEVITABILITY OF CHALLENGES

The path to peace, like any journey, is not without its bumps and curves. In its unpredictable nature, life throws challenges our way, testing our resolve and threatening our hard-earned tranquility. These are not obstacles to be feared or avoided but rather opportunities to deepen our understanding of peace and strengthen our inner resilience.

Imagine a majestic mountain range, its peaks reaching towards the heavens. Reaching the summit is the ultimate goal, but the ascent is challenging. Steep inclines, rocky trails, and unpredictable weather conditions test the climber's fortitude. Yet, in the face of these obstacles, true strength and resilience are forged.

Similarly, our journey to inner peace is not a smooth, linear path. We encounter moments of doubt, fear, anger, and sorrow – storms that threaten to engulf us in their tumultuous waves. These are the inevitable trials that test our commitment to peace. During these challenging times, we must remember that inner peace is not a destination to be reached but a state of being to be cultivated.

During these challenging times, we must remember that inner peace is not a destination to be reached but a state of being to be cultivated. Think of it as a muscle we continuously strengthen through practice and perseverance. We learn to navigate these storms with composure, remaining grounded in our center even when the world seems to be falling apart.

Navigating these turbulent waters requires a change in our perception. We must learn to embrace the challenges, not as threats but as opportunities for growth. Each setback, each moment of adversity, is a chance to refine our inner strength and deepen our connection to the source of peace within. Just as a skilled sailor uses the wind and waves to navigate the ocean, we can use our challenges to refine our inner compass and guide us toward a greater sense of serenity.

The power of resilience lies in our ability to bounce back, rise above adversity, and maintain our inner equilibrium. We are not defined by the storms we encounter but by how we weather them. Our ability to remain steadfast in the face of challenges is a testament to the strength and resilience we cultivate on our journey to peace.

This journey requires constant practice and a willingness to evolve. It is not about denying or ignoring the challenges but about learning to face them with courage and wisdom. Through mindful awareness, we learn to recognize the fleeting nature of difficult emotions, allowing them to pass through us without clinging to them. This is the essence of inner peace – the ability to remain grounded and present amid turmoil.

Imagine a serene lake, its surface reflecting the clear blue sky. The occasional ripples on the water, caused by a gentle breeze or a falling leaf, do not disturb the underlying stillness of the lake. In the same way, we can cultivate an inner stillness that remains undisturbed by the waves of life's challenges.

Remember, peace is not the absence of challenges but the presence of inner strength and resilience. It is the ability to weather the storms, embrace life's inevitable ups and downs, and emerge from each challenge with a renewed sense of peace. Embrace the journey, cultivate your inner strength, and navigate life's challenges with grace and serenity. Within each challenge lies an opportunity to deepen your connection to the source of peace within you.

Resilience is the bedrock of inner peace, the unwavering strength that allows us to weather life's inevitable storms with grace and composure. It's not about denying the pain or pretending everything is perfect. It's about recognizing the reality of hardship, accepting it with courage, and finding the inner resources to rise above it. Think of it as a deep wellspring of strength within you, always available to draw upon when life throws you curveballs.

Imagine a mighty oak tree, rooted deep in the earth, standing tall against the winds and storms. It bends, it sways, but it never breaks. That's resilience in action. Just as the oak tree draws strength from its roots, our resilience comes from our core values, beliefs, and connection to something bigger than ourselves.

Life is filled with ups and downs, joy and sorrow, triumphs and setbacks. It's the nature of existence. But how we respond to these experiences determines our inner peace and well-being. Resilience isn't about avoiding challenges but navigating them with a sense of strength and unwavering spirit.

Here's the key to building resilience:

**Embrace Impermanence:** One of the most important lessons we can learn is that nothing is permanent. Life is constantly in flux, and clinging to outcomes or fearing change only creates anxiety and fear. Embrace the natural flow of life, knowing that challenges, just like joys, are temporary.

**Cultivate a Growth Mindset:** View challenges not as obstacles but as opportunities for growth. Every difficult situation is a chance to learn, adapt, and emerge stronger. Remember, resilience is about bouncing back, not just surviving. It's about becoming a better, more adaptable version of yourself.

**Find Your Anchor:** What are the things that ground you? This could be your faith, loved ones, passions, or a deeply held belief system. When you're facing hardship, these anchors provide stability and support. Lean on them during difficult times, and you'll find the strength to persevere.

**Practice Self-Compassion:** It's easy to be hard on yourself during tough times. But remember, everyone struggles. Be kind to yourself, forgive your mistakes, and offer yourself the compassion you would offer a dear friend. Self-compassion is essential for resilience, allowing you to heal and move forward with renewed hope.

Let's look at some real-life examples of resilience in action:

**The Athlete Overcoming Injury:** Imagine a professional athlete who has dedicated their life to their sport. They've trained tirelessly, made sacrifices, and dreamed of achieving greatness. Then, suddenly, they suffer a debilitating injury that threatens their career. This is an actual test of resilience. Will they wallow in despair, or will they find the strength to overcome the adversity? The resilient athlete uses this setback as an opportunity to learn, grow, and return more vital than ever. They may have to change their training methods, find new ways to push their limits or develop a new perspective on their sport. But through it all, they maintain their focus and their determination.

**The Entrepreneur Facing Failure:** Starting a business is risky, and most entrepreneurs will experience setbacks along the way. They might face financial challenges, competition, or unexpected market changes. These obstacles can be disheartening, and some might give up. However, the resilient entrepreneur sees these challenges as learning opportunities. They adapt, learn from their mistakes, and persevere, eventually achieving success. Their resilience is fueled by their passion, their commitment, and their belief in their vision.

**The Individual Facing Loss:** Loss is a universal human experience that can be incredibly painful. The death of a loved one, the end of a relationship, or a job loss can leave us feeling shattered. But the resilient individual finds a way to grieve, heal, and move forward. They lean on their support systems, practice self-care, and find ways to honor the memories of what they've lost. Resilience in the face of loss is about finding meaning in the experience, learning from it, and allowing it to shape you into a stronger, more compassionate person.

Remember, resilience is not about being invincible. It's about recognizing that we're human, that we'll face challenges, and that we can find the strength to overcome them. It's about learning to embrace life's ups and downs, find meaning in our experiences, and emerge more robust and peaceful on the other side.

Embrace your resilience. It's a gift that will serve you well throughout your life, guiding you to inner peace and a sense of enduring strength.

In its intricate tapestry, life is woven with threads of joy and sorrow, triumph and tribulation. Through the lens of these challenges, the seeming "downs" in our journey, we discover the profound depth of our resilience and the transformative power of inner peace. While we may long for a life devoid of difficulties, it is precisely in the face of adversity that we unveil our true potential and deepen our connection to the tranquil space within.

Think of a sturdy oak tree, its roots deeply embedded in the earth. It has weathered countless storms, each tempestuous wind testing its strength and forging its resilience. The oak doesn't merely survive these trials; it thrives, becoming more grounded and expansive. Similarly, when embraced with an open heart and a discerning mind, our challenges become the fertile ground for our growth and the catalyst for deepening our inner peace.

The path to peace is a challenging road. It's a winding journey, at times difficult, but ultimately leading to a profound transformation. When we encounter difficulties, it's easy to fall into the trap of negativity, allowing our thoughts to spiral downward and fueling fear, frustration, or despair. However, in these moments of discomfort, we can rise above the storm to cultivate a more profound sense of stability and inner strength.

Imagine a ship navigating a tumultuous sea. As waves crash against its hull, the ship's captain remains steadfast, skillfully steering the vessel through the turbulence. They don't fight the storm; they work with it, adjusting their course and utilizing the natural forces to maintain stability. Our challenges are like these waves, testing our composure and requiring us to tap into our inner reserves of wisdom and strength.

This isn't about ignoring or minimizing the pain and difficulty we may experience. It's about recognizing the inherent opportunity within each challenge, the chance to learn, grow, and deepen our understanding of ourselves and the world around us. Each obstacle we overcome, each hardship we weather, adds another layer of strength to our inner fortress, allowing us to stand tall even when the winds of adversity blow strong.

Here's how to view challenges as opportunities:

**Shifting Perspective:** When faced with a difficulty, pause, take a deep breath, and ask yourself, "What can I learn from this? How can I grow through this experience?" This shift in perspective allows us to move from a reactive state to a more contemplative, even compassionate, approach.

**Embrace the Learning Curve:** Challenges are often disguised opportunities for learning and growth. They allow us to develop new skills, strengthen our resilience, and discover hidden strengths we may have never known we possessed. Each challenge, when approached with a growth mindset, becomes a valuable lesson in our journey of self-discovery.

**Practicing Compassion:** When facing challenges, it's easy to turn inward, focusing on our discomfort. However, extending compassion to ourselves and others during these times can be incredibly powerful. It allows us to acknowledge our feelings without judgment, creating a space for acceptance and understanding.

The journey of peace isn't about escaping the storms of life. It's about learning to navigate them with grace, wisdom, and resilience. It's about finding inner calm amidst the chaos and the unwavering stillness of the hurricane. As we cultivate this internal strength, we weather the storms of life with greater ease and emerge more grounded, more resilient, and more deeply connected to the profound peace that resides within us all.

The journey to peace is not a linear path; it's a winding road with its share of bumps and detours. In its rich tapestry, life presents us with moments of joy and ease alongside challenges and setbacks. While we strive for inner harmony, we cannot shy away from the inevitable storms that life throws us. In these challenging moments, the actual currency of peace shines its brightest. Maintaining a positive outlook during these times is not about pretending difficulties don't exist but about shifting our perspective, embracing resilience, and remembering the inherent goodness that permeates even the darkest nights.

Imagine a mighty oak tree standing tall against the wind. Its roots, firmly anchored in the earth, draw strength from the very ground it stands upon. Likewise, when life's storms rage around us, we can find our grounding in gratitude, hope, and unwavering belief in our inherent capacity for resilience. This is where the power of a positive outlook truly unfolds.

### The Gratitude Lens:

Gratitude is a powerful antidote to negativity. When we focus on what we have rather than what we lack, a sense of contentment washes over us. Even in the midst of hardship, there are always things to be grateful for – the sun's warmth on our skin, the love of family and friends, and the strength within us. Start a gratitude journal, a simple notebook where you jot down three daily things you're thankful for. These could be as grand as a breathtaking sunset or as small as a cup of tea that brings a moment of peace.

By focusing on these positive aspects, we shift our perspective, fostering a more optimistic outlook.

### *Hope: The Guiding Light:*

Hope is a flickering flame that sustains us through dark times. It's the belief that things will eventually get better and that a brighter future is waiting to be unveiled. When we cultivate hope, we open ourselves to possibilities, believing that even in the face of adversity, we can find a path forward. Hope is not wishful thinking; it's a conscious choice to believe in the goodness of life, even when it seems distant.

Hope isn't always a grand gesture; it can be found in minor actions. Knowing it holds the potential for new life, planting a seed in the garden is a tangible expression of hope. Sharing a kind word with a stranger, a small act of kindness, carries the promise of a better world within it. Each act of hope, no matter how small, adds to the collective energy of positivity and builds a foundation for a brighter future.

### *The Inherent Goodness of Life:*

Even when faced with adversity, we must never forget the inherent goodness of life. This goodness exists in the simple things – the laughter of a child, the beauty of a sunrise, the unwavering love of a pet. It's the kindness of strangers, the resilience of the human spirit, and the power of nature to heal and renew.

In its wisdom, the universe offers us an abundance of beauty, wonder, and love. Even amid darkness, these elements are always present, waiting to be discovered. It's our choice to focus on these aspects, to see the world through a lens of hope and appreciation, even when faced with hardship.

### *Embracing Resilience:*

Resilience is not about ignoring challenges but about learning to navigate them with grace and strength. It's about accepting that life is a journey, not a destination, and challenges are inevitable. It's about acknowledging our emotions, allowing ourselves to feel the pain of setbacks, and then rising above them with renewed determination.

Resilience is a muscle that can be strengthened through practice. When faced with a challenge, take a moment to breathe deeply, acknowledge your feelings, and remind yourself of your inherent strength. Seek support from loved ones, engage in activities that bring you joy, and remind yourself that you can overcome.

### *A Journey of Continuous Growth:*

Maintaining a positive outlook is not a one-time event; it's an ongoing practice. It's about being mindful of our thoughts and focusing on gratitude, hope, and the inherent goodness of life, even when faced with challenges. It's about learning from our experiences, embracing resilience, and cultivating inner peace.

# THE CURRENCY OF PEACE

The path to peace is a journey of continuous growth and self-discovery. It's about embracing the ups and downs of life, knowing that even amid difficulties, there is always a reason to hope, a reason to believe in the beauty of life, and a reason to keep moving forward with a positive and open heart. Like a precious gem, the currency of peace shines its brightest in the darkest moments. Embrace this inner strength, and watch as it transforms your life and the world around you.

The journey to lasting peace is not a destination but an ongoing process, a continuous dance of self-awareness, practice, and commitment. It's like tending a garden – the seeds of peace are sown within us, but they require constant nurturing, weeding out negative thoughts and emotions, and providing the right conditions for growth.

Think of it as a winding path, a gradual unfolding of inner harmony. There will be moments of serenity and joy where your cultivated peace feels profound and unshakeable. But there will also be times of turmoil and struggle when the shadows of doubt, fear, or anger threaten to engulf you. This is where your commitment to the journey becomes crucial.

Remember, every challenge you face, and every obstacle you overcome deepens your understanding of peace and strengthens your resilience. In these moments of adversity, you learn the true meaning of inner peace, the ability to remain centered amidst the storms of life.

The path to lasting peace requires daily practice. Just as we brush our teeth every morning, we must ignore the negative thoughts and emotions that cloud our minds. This is where practices like meditation, mindfulness, and deep breathing come in. They provide a sanctuary where you can connect with your inner self, observe your thoughts and feelings without judgment, and cultivate a sense of calm and serenity.

However, the practice of peace extends beyond formal meditation sessions. It's about bringing awareness to every moment of your day, every interaction you have, every thought that arises. It's about choosing compassion over judgment, forgiveness over resentment, and love over fear.

The path to peace is also about letting go of attachment and expectations. We often create our suffering by clinging to outcomes, people, or things that ultimately don't bring us lasting happiness. Learning to let go, to accept things as they are, and to trust in the unfolding of life is essential for inner peace.

The journey to lasting peace is not about achieving a perfect state of tranquility; it's about embracing the ebb and flow of life, the ups and downs, the joys and sorrows. It's about finding balance and harmony within yourself, a place of peace, no matter what life throws your way. It's about cultivating a sense of inner strength, a resilience that allows you to navigate life's challenges with grace, compassion, and an unwavering belief in the power of peace.

As you continue on this journey, you may encounter moments of doubt, frustration, or even despair. Don't be discouraged. These are simply signposts along the path, guiding you toward a deeper understanding of yourself and a more profound experience of peace. Remember, you're not alone on this journey. Countless others have traveled this path before you, and innumerable resources and communities are available to support you.

The journey to peace is a lifelong endeavor, but it's a journey worth taking. The rewards are immeasurable – a sense of inner harmony, a greater capacity for love and compassion, a deeper connection with your true self, and a life of purpose and meaning. In a world that often feels chaotic and turbulent, the presence of peace within you can create a ripple effect of positivity that extends outward, inspiring others to embark on their own journeys of peace and creating a more loving, compassionate, and harmonious world.

# 10

## THE CURRENCY OF PEACE: A LEGACY OF TRANQULITY

Imagine a world where anger and hostility are replaced by compassion and understanding, fear gives way to courage, and conflict dissolves into collaboration. This is the world that emerges when inner peace becomes the foundation of our individual lives, our relationships, and our communities.

When we cultivate inner peace, we unlock a transformative power that extends far beyond our experiences. It becomes a catalyst for positive change, radiating outwards to touch the lives of those around us. This ripple effect of peace begins with a shift in our perception, a conscious choice to embrace calmness and tranquility amidst the storms of life.

As we learn to quiet the constant chatter of our minds, manage our emotions with grace, and respond to challenges with wisdom and compassion, we create a space for peace to flourish. This inner sanctuary becomes a haven from the anxieties and stresses that plague our modern world. It allows us to connect with our true selves, tap into our innate wisdom, and experience joy, contentment, and fulfillment independent of external circumstances.

This newfound peace doesn't simply bring solace to our own lives; it transforms our relationships with others. When we approach interactions with a peaceful mindset, we create an atmosphere of understanding, respect, and genuine connection. The barriers of judgment, prejudice, and resentment crumble, replaced by a genuine desire to connect and collaborate. This interaction shift extends beyond our relationships, impacting our communities, workplaces, and even the world.

Think of a family where parents have cultivated inner peace. Their children, witnessing the calm amidst chaos, learn to navigate their emotions with more excellent composure and empathy. This ripple effect continues as those children grow into adulthood, bringing peace into their families and communities.

In the same way, consider a workplace where employees prioritize inner peace. Conflict resolution becomes more harmonious, communication is more effective, and creativity is more abundant. This fosters a more positive and productive environment, benefiting the employees, the organization, and stakeholders.

On a global scale, the impact of inner peace is even more profound. When individuals embrace peace within themselves, they become beacons of hope and agents of change in a world often plagued by conflict and violence. These individuals become advocates for understanding, forgiveness, and reconciliation. They dedicate themselves to building bridges across divides, fostering collaboration, and promoting solutions that address the root causes of conflict.

The collective impact of countless individuals living a life of peace is immeasurable. It creates a world where dialogue replaces violence, collaboration replaces competition, and harmony prevails. This is not a utopian dream but a tangible reality we can make, one heart at a time, by embracing the power of inner peace and its transformative potential.

The journey to peace can be challenging. We will encounter challenges, setbacks, and moments of doubt. But the reward is worth the effort. Cultivating inner peace is a journey of self-discovery, a path that leads to a more fulfilling, meaningful, and peaceful life. It is a gift we can give ourselves and a legacy we can leave for future generations.

As we embark on this journey, we may find that peace is not a destination but a way of life. It is a constant practice, a commitment to cultivating a peaceful mindset, managing our emotions gracefully, and extending compassion to ourselves and others.

In the tapestry of human existence, each thread of inner peace contributes to a larger pattern of harmony and well-being. Let us choose to weave our threads of peace, creating a tapestry of tranquility that will inspire generations to come.

The journey to inner peace is not just a personal pursuit; it's a gift we can share with the world. The peace we cultivate within ourselves has the power to ripple outwards, impacting our relationships, our communities, and the world at large. By sharing the principles and practices of inner peace, we become ambassadors of tranquility, spreading a message of hope, understanding, and well-being.

Imagine a world where everyone had access to the tools for cultivating inner peace. Imagine a world where conflict was resolved through understanding and empathy, compassion replaced judgment, and kindness reigned supreme. This is the power of sharing the gift of peace.

But how do we share this gift? How do we inspire others to embark on their journeys towards inner peace? It starts with our example. By embodying the principles of peace in our daily lives, we become living embodiments of tranquility. Our actions, words, and thoughts become a silent message to those around us, demonstrating the power of peace in action.

We can also share our knowledge and experiences. We can inspire others to explore the path to inner peace through conversations, workshops, and written words. We can share the tools and techniques we've learned, such as meditation, mindfulness, and deep breathing exercises, empowering them to cultivate their sense of inner harmony.

Furthermore, we can actively create a culture of peace within our communities. This might involve advocating for peaceful solutions to conflict, promoting understanding and empathy, or treating everyone with kindness and respect. Our actions, however small, can contribute to building a more peaceful and compassionate world.

Sharing the gift of peace is not just about spreading a message; it's about creating a ripple effect of positive change. When we help others find peace within themselves, we create a domino effect that spreads outward, impacting countless lives. This is the true power of sharing the gift of peace—it's not just about words but about transforming lives, one peaceful heart at a time.

Here are some practical ways to share the gift of peace:

**Lead by example:** Be the peace you want to see. Live a life guided by the principles of peace: kindness, compassion, empathy, and forgiveness.

**Share your story:** Tell others about your journey to inner peace. Share the challenges you've faced and the tools that have helped you.

**Offer resources:** Introduce others to books, articles, websites, and courses on cultivating inner peace. Share your favorite practices and techniques for finding tranquility.

**Start a conversation:** Initiate conversations about peace and well-being. Ask others about their experiences and share your insights.

**Practice active listening:** Listen to others with empathy and understanding. Offer a listening ear and a supportive presence.

**Be a peacemaker:** In the face of conflict, strive to be a mediator, encouraging understanding and compassion.

**Support peace organizations:** Donate to or volunteer for organizations promoting peace and well-being globally.

Remember, the journey to peace is a personal one. Still, it's also a collective endeavor. By sharing the gift of peace, we contribute to a world where kindness, understanding, and compassion prevail. We create a world where peace is not just a dream but a reality, built on the foundation of countless peaceful hearts. Let us all strive to be beacons of peace, sharing the gift of tranquility and inspiring others to find their inner oasis of peace.

Material possessions or accomplishments do not merely measure the legacy we leave behind but also the impact we have on the world and the ripples of peace and harmony we set in motion. Cultivating inner peace is not a selfish pursuit; it's a powerful act of generosity that extends far beyond ourselves. By embracing the principles and practices of peace within, we become beacons of tranquility, illuminating the path for future generations.

Imagine a world where children are raised in homes where peace reigns, disagreements are resolved with compassion and understanding, and love and kindness are the guiding principles. This is the legacy we can create when we prioritize inner peace. It's not about achieving perfect serenity but nurturing a resilient spirit, an inner strength that allows us to weather life's storms with grace and composure.

Our journey to inner peace is not just about our well-being; it's about becoming a force for good in the world. When we respond to anger with understanding, fear with courage, and negativity with kindness, we inspire those around us to do the same. We become living examples of the power of peace, demonstrating that true strength lies not in dominance but in the capacity for empathy and forgiveness.

The legacy of peace we create is not confined to our immediate families and communities. It extends outward, reaching generations yet to come. By sharing the tools and techniques we've learned on our journey to inner peace, we empower others to navigate their challenges with greater resilience and serenity.

This legacy is not about imposing our beliefs or practices on others but offering a guiding light, a beacon of hope in a world often consumed by conflict and turmoil. It's about sharing that peace is not an unattainable ideal but a state of being that can be cultivated within each of us.

How do we leave this legacy of peace? It starts with our commitment to the journey. We must continue to explore our inner landscape, uncovering the sources of our inner turmoil and replacing them with practices that nurture peace. This may include meditation, mindfulness, gratitude practices, deep breathing techniques, or any other practice that helps us connect with the tranquility that resides within.

The next step is sharing our journey with others. We can do this through our actions, words, and presence. By embodying peace in our daily interactions, we inspire those around us to seek it in their lives. We can also share our knowledge and insights through conversations, workshops, or writing.

A legacy of peace is not about achieving something monumental or making grand pronouncements. It's about the quiet, persistent commitment to living a life that radiates peace and inspires others to do the same. It's about recognizing that true peace begins within and is a gift we can share with the world, leaving a lasting imprint of tranquility for generations to come.

Consider these steps as you embark on creating a legacy of peace:

**Be a role model:** Let your life be an example of inner peace. Live with kindness, compassion, and empathy, demonstrating the power of peace in action.

**Share your story:** Talk about your journey to inner peace. Share the challenges you've faced, the lessons you've learned, and the practices that have helped you find peace.

**Educate and inspire:** Share your knowledge and insights through writing, teaching, or mentoring. Help others discover the path to inner peace and its transformative power.

**Live a life of purpose:** Align your actions with your values and purpose. By pursuing your passion and positively contributing to the world, you embody the principles of peace and inspire others to do the same.

We can all contribute to a legacy of peace by taking these steps. This legacy transcends the boundaries of time and place, creating a more peaceful and harmonious world for future generations.

The promise of peace lies not in a distant utopia but in the very fabric of our being. Inner peace, once cultivated, becomes a wellspring of tranquility, radiating outwards to touch every aspect of our lives and the world around us. It's a transformation that begins within, a subtle shift in consciousness that ripples outwards, creating a more harmonious and loving world.

Imagine a world where anger gives way to understanding, fear yields courage, and hatred is replaced by compassion. This isn't a fantasy; it's the potential that unfolds when we embrace the power of inner peace. The quiet strength that arises from within becomes a beacon of hope, illuminating the path toward a more peaceful future.

We are not passive bystanders in this journey. Each of us holds the potential to cultivate inner peace and, in doing so, contribute to a more peaceful world. It's a collective effort, a symphony of individual transformations, that can create a world where conflict is replaced by cooperation, division is replaced by unity, and whole violence is replaced by love.

The world we yearn for peace and harmony begins with each of us. It starts with the conscious choice to cultivate inner tranquility, prioritize our well-being, and extend that peace to others. It's about recognizing that true peace is not the absence of conflict but the presence of a profound, enduring tranquility that resides within us, waiting to be awakened.

This is not about ignoring the world's challenges but confronting them with a heart full of peace. It's about understanding that actual change begins with ourselves. When we cultivate inner peace, we become agents of change, inspiring those around us to do the same.

Think of a single drop of water. It may seem insignificant, but when it falls into a larger body of water, it creates a ripple effect that spreads throughout the entire surface. Likewise, each act of cultivating inner peace creates a ripple effect, touching the lives of others and spreading a sense of harmony and well-being.

This is the promise of peace – the power to transform ourselves and the world. It's a journey that requires courage, commitment, and a willingness to embrace the transformative power within each of us. It's a journey worth taking, for the rewards are immeasurable, not only for ourselves but for all we touch.

The journey to inner peace is a lifelong adventure that unfolds with every step we take, every breath we draw, and every moment we choose to live with intention. It's not a destination to be reached but a state of being to cultivate, a practice to embrace. It is about recognizing that true peace resides within us, waiting to be discovered and nurtured.

Think of inner peace as a garden. It requires tending, nurturing, and consistent care. It thrives when we cultivate mindfulness, self-awareness, and compassion. It wilts in the shadow of negativity, fear, and judgment. The journey to inner peace is about tending this garden, weeding out the negativity, and planting seeds of love, kindness, and forgiveness.

Remember, the journey can be challenging. There will be storms, droughts, and challenges. But with each obstacle we overcome, our resilience grows stronger. With each act of compassion, our hearts open wider. With each moment of mindful awareness, we learn to navigate the ebbs and flows of life with grace and poise.

Embrace the ups and downs, the triumphs and setbacks, as opportunities for growth. Through these experiences, we truly learn the meaning of peace, not as a static state but as a dynamic and ever-evolving process.

The path to inner peace is a path of self-discovery, a journey of rediscovering our inherent worth, our connection to something larger than ourselves. It is about learning to listen to the whispers of our souls, trusting the Holy Spirit, or intuition, and aligning our lives with our deepest values.

As you embark on this journey, remember that you are not alone. There is a vast community of seekers, just like you, yearning for peace and harmony. Connect with like-minded individuals, share your experiences, and support each other in this transformative endeavor.

Cultivating inner peace is a gift you give not only to yourself but to the world. When we find peace within, we radiate it outward, touching the lives of those around us. We become beacons of hope, catalysts for change, and ambassadors of a more peaceful and harmonious world.

The journey to inner peace is a worthy and rewarding pursuit, a testament to the resilience of the human spirit. It is a journey of self-discovery, healing, and transformation, leading to a life filled with purpose, joy, and profound inner tranquility. Embrace the journey, trust the process, and know that you are moving closer to the peace within you with each step.

# ACKNOWLEDGMENTS

First and foremost, I want to thank God for His immeasurable grace, guidance, and strength in completing this book. His love is the foundation of every peaceful relationship, and I am eternally grateful for His presence in my life. To Him be the glory for the wisdom shared here.

I am deeply grateful to my spiritual mentor, Pleased Prophet Friday Ibanga, for his encouragement, prayers, and the wisdom he has imparted to me throughout my journey. His support has been instrumental in shaping my spiritual growth and my ministry.

I want to thank Dr. Pat Akpabio for her guidance, leadership, and constant inspiration. Her commitment to seeing me succeed has meant more than words can express.

To Margaret Ogunmefun, Dr. Debbie Obatoki, and Mr. Richard Frank, I am forever grateful for your unwavering support, advice, and encouragement. You have all played a vital role in this journey, and I cherish each of you.

I want to thank Tonya Larana for her invaluable contribution and Felicia Brown for her unwavering support throughout this journey.

Your encouragement and dedication have been instrumental in bringing this project to life.

I sincerely thank Prophet Frank Udoh for his unwavering support throughout this journey. I am deeply grateful for your role in helping me fulfill my purpose. Thank you for standing with me in faith and believing in this project's vision. May God continue to bless you and elevate your ministry.

Lastly, I want to acknowledge all those who have contributed to this work in some way, whether by sharing their stories, offering prayers, or providing feedback. This book results from a collective effort, and I thank you all from my heart.

# APPENDIX

## Additional Resources for Deepening Your Exploration of Peace

This appendix provides additional resources that can help you further explore and cultivate peace in various aspects of your life—internally, relationally, and spiritually. These resources include books, tools, and practices designed to support your personal journey of growth and fulfillment.

## Books:

1. **"The Universe in a Single Atom: The Convergence of Science and Spirituality" by His Holiness the Dalai Lama**
   This book blends scientific and spiritual insights, offering a unique perspective on inner peace and balance between mind, body, and spirit.

2. **"The Book of Joy: Lasting Happiness in a Changing World" by Dalai Lama and Desmond Tutu**

A dialogue between two of the world's most respected spiritual leaders, this book offers practical advice on how to cultivate joy and peace, especially during life's challenges.

3. **"Peace is Every Step: The Path of Mindfulness in Everyday Life" by Thich Nhat Hanh**
This book is a practical guide to mindfulness. It explores how to create peace in daily life through conscious awareness and compassion.

4. **"The Anatomy of Peace: Resolving the Heart of Conflict" by The Arbinger Institute**
This book presents tools for resolving conflicts, offering strategies for creating peace in relationships and communities.

5. **"Inner Engineering: A Yogi's Guide to Joy" by Sadhguru**
A holistic guide to achieving inner peace, this book offers spiritual practices to align the body, mind, and spirit for a life of fulfillment and joy.

## Meditation and Mindfulness Tools:

- **Headspace**: An app that provides guided meditations and mindfulness exercises to help you reduce stress and find inner peace.

Website: www.headspace.com

- **Calm** is another meditation app that offers relaxation techniques, guided meditations, and sleep aids to foster mental peace and emotional well-being.
Website: www.calm.com

## Holistic Health Practices:

- **Yoga with Adriene** (YouTube Channel): A free resource for practicing yoga at home, promoting physical and emotional balance.
Website: Yoga with Adriene

- **The Heart Math Institute**: Provides tools and research to help you balance emotions and reduce stress for a peaceful heart and mind.
Website: www.heartmath.org

## Supportive Communities:

- **Peace One Day**: An initiative dedicated to promoting peace and reducing violence worldwide, offering resources and events to encourage global harmony.
Website: www.peaceoneday.org

- **The Global Peace Index**: A resource providing insights and data on peace levels around the world, offering valuable information for understanding global peace efforts. Website: www.visionofhumanity.org

# Glossary

This glossary defines key terms used in the book:

**Attachment:**

Emotional or psychological dependence on something or someone can lead to suffering and a lack of inner peace.

**Compassion:**

The ability to understand and share the feelings of others leads to empathy and a desire to help.

**Empathy:**

The capacity to understand and share another person's feelings, putting yourself in their shoes.

**Forgiveness:**

Letting go of resentment, anger, and bitterness toward yourself or others allows for healing and inner peace.

**Intuition:**

A gut feeling or inner knowing provides guidance and wisdom beyond conscious thought.

**Mindfulness:**

The practice of being fully present in the current moment, paying attention to thoughts, feelings, and sensations without judgment.

**Purpose:**

The reason for your existence, your unique contribution to the world, and the driving force behind your actions.

**Resilience:**

The ability to bounce back from adversity, maintain inner peace in the face of challenges, and adapt to changing circumstances.

**Spirit:**

The essence of your being, connection to a higher power, and the source of your inner strength and wisdom.

**Visualization:**

The practice of creating mental images of desired outcomes, aligning thoughts and actions with your intentions.

This glossary is intended to provide a deeper understanding of the concepts presented in the book.

## Author Biography

Paul Frank is a life coach, public speaker, and evangelist dedicated to helping individuals cultivate peace and meaningful relationships in all areas of life. With over a decade of experience in coaching, Paul has guided countless individuals and couples toward emotional healing and spiritual growth through his unique blend of practical strategies and faith-based principles.

In *The Currency of Peace*, Paul draws on his journey of faith and mentorship from spiritual leaders like Prophet Friday Ibanga to explore peace as a precious, irreplaceable commodity that transcends money. Through his work, he emphasizes the importance of achieving inner peace by harmonizing the body, soul, and spirit and extending that peace into relationships, communities, and every aspect of life.

As the founder of Triple O Foundation, Paul promotes connection across business, health, relationships, and community. The foundation's mission is centered around the slogan "One World, One Life, One Connect." His life's work is devoted to helping others discover their purpose, live fulfilling lives, and foster peaceful connections with themselves and others.

Paul resides in Texas, where he continues to inspire, teach, and empower through his ministry and coaching. When he isn't coaching or speaking, he enjoys writing, expanding his knowledge of holistic health, and working on new projects that promote peace and well-being across the globe.

Made in the USA
Middletown, DE
08 February 2025

70599959R00110